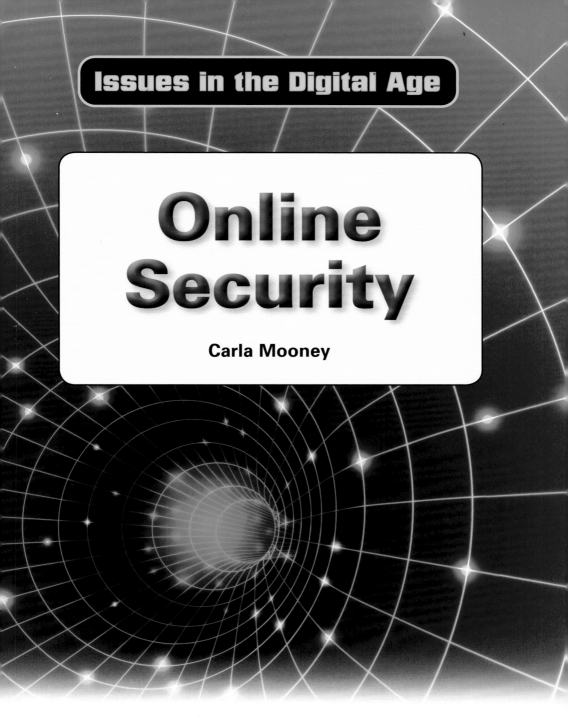

Issues in the Digital Age

Online Security

Carla Mooney

ReferencePoint
Press®

San Diego, CA

© 2012 ReferencePoint Press, Inc.
Printed in the United States

For more information, contact:
ReferencePoint Press, Inc.
PO Box 27779
San Diego, CA 92198
www. ReferencePointPress.com

LIBRARY OF CONGRESS CATALOGING-IN-PUBLICATION DATA

Mooney, Carla, 1970–
  Online security / by Carla Mooney.
    p. cm. — (Issues in the digital age series)
  Includes bibliographical references and index.
  ISBN-13: 978-1-60152-195-8 (hardback)
  ISBN-10: 1-60152-195-2 (hardback)
  1. Computer networks—Security measures—Juvenile literature. 2. Computer crimes—Juvenile literature. I. Title.
  TK5105.59.M65 2012
  364.16'8—dc23
                                                                                                2011022438

Contents

Introduction

Data Breach

On March 14, 2011, Health Net, a California-based managed health care organization, announced that it had launched an investigation into several computer server drives that were missing from its data center in Rancho Cordova, California. Health Net executives became aware of the missing drives when IBM, the vendor responsible for managing Health Net's information technology (IT) systems, notified them that they could not locate the drives. The drives contained personal information for 1.9 million current and former Health Net customers, including names, addresses, Social Security numbers, health information, and financial information. "Based on the information we have compiled, this is among the top 20 security breaches (nationwide) since 2005," says Beth Givens, director of Privacy Rights Clearinghouse, a San Diego nonprofit consumer organization. "This is a very large breach of very sensitive information."[1]

The Health Net data breach could prove to be extremely costly for the affected customers and the company. If personal information falls into the wrong hands, customers could become victims of identity theft. Identity theft occurs when someone uses another individual's personal information, typically for financial gain. According to the 2010 US Consumer Study by IdentityHawk, a company that provides identity protection services, identity theft costs about $4,800 per victim. This estimate does not include the countless hours spent by victims to resolve credit and fraud issues. In addition, a study by the Ponemon Institute, a research organization that studies information security, and Symantec Corporation, an Internet security company, found that data breaches cost companies $214 per affected person. This average cost includes expenses for lost business, investigations, legal services, customer contacts, and identity protection services.

What made the Health Net breach more problematic is that the information contained on the missing drives was not encrypted. Encrypted data is translated into a secret code. To read it a user must have a key or password to decode it. Many companies and users encrypt sensitive data to prevent it from being read by unauthorized people. Givens says Health Net could have taken a few simple steps to avoid such a large data breach. "The fact that a server drive is unaccounted for is astounding," she says. "Under California law, this wouldn't even be a breach if the data had been encrypted. And relative to the expense of notifying affected individuals, (encrypting records) is not expensive."[2]

Increasing Need for Online Security

In a relatively short period of time, Internet and digital technology have revolutionized the way people around the world communicate and conduct business. Digital technology enables businesses like Health Net to store millions of records electronically on hard drives and other digital devices. In addition, the globally connected online network known as the Internet allows the average person to have unprecedented access to all sorts of information. Using computers or other digital devices that communicate through the Internet, people can send messages, bank, shop, or search for information from anywhere at any time.

Yet as electronic data storage and online connections multiply, there is an increasing risk that valuable information could be lost, stolen, or changed. One employee can mistakenly send a file with confidential information to an entire e-mail distribution list. Other times, online criminals infect users' computers with viruses and spyware that enable them to steal personal information. With this information, they can commit financial fraud or identity theft.

Cybercriminals also hack into corporate computer systems, stealing databases of customer information or corporate secrets. Other times, cyberspies and terrorists use the Internet and digital technology to disrupt the operation of websites, companies, and governments. Pam Dixon,

> "Once files are in electronic form, the crime scales up quickly. There are cases where someone has walked out with thousands and thousands of files on a thumb drive. You can't do that with paper files."[3]
>
> — Pam Dixon, founder of the World Privacy Forum, a non-profit consumer-research group.

Online Activities by Age

Ages 18–33	Ages 34–45	Ages 46–55	Ages 56–64	Ages 65–73	Ages 74+
E-mail	E-mail	E-mail	E-mail	E-mail	E-mail
Search	Search	Search	Search	Search	Search
Health info	Health info	Health info	Health info	Health info	Health info
Social network sites	Get news	Get news	Get news	Get news	Buy a product
Watch video	Gov't website	Gov't website	Gov't website	Travel reservations	Get news
Get news	Travel reservations	Travel reservations	Buy a product	Buy a product	Travel reservations
Buy a product	Watch video	Buy a product	Travel reservations	Gov't website	Gov't website
IM	Buy a product	Watch video	Bank online	Watch video	Bank online
Listen to music	Social network sites	Bank online	Watch video	Financial info	Financial info
Travel reservations	Bank online	Social network sites	Social network sites	Bank online	Religious info
Online classifieds	Online classifieds	Online classifieds	Online classifieds	Rate things	Watch video
Bank online	Listen to music	Listen to music	Financial info	Social network sites	Play games
Gov't website	IM	Financial info	Rate things	Online classifieds	Online classifieds
Play games	Play games	IM	Listen to music	IM	Social network sites
Read blogs	Financial info	Religious info	Religious info	Religious info	Rate things
Financial info	Religious info	Rate things	IM	Play games	Read blogs
Rate things	Read blogs	Read blogs	Play games	Listen to music	Donate to charity
Religious info	Rate things	Play games	Read blogs	Read blogs	Listen to music
Online auction	Online auction	Online auction	Online auction	Donate to charity	Podcasts
Podcasts	Donate to charity	Donate to charity	Donate to charity	Online auction	Online auction
Donate to charity	Podcasts	Podcasts	Podcasts	Podcasts	Blog
Blog	Blog	Blog	Blog	Blog	IM
Virtual worlds	Virtual worlds	Virtual worlds	Virtual worlds	Virtual worlds	Virtual worlds

Source: Pew Internet & American Life Project, "Generations 2010: What Different Generations Do Online," December 16, 2010. www.pewinternet.org.

founder of the World Privacy Forum, a nonprofit consumer-research group, says: "Once files are in electronic form, the crime scales up quickly. There are cases where someone has walked out with thousands and thousands of files on a thumb drive. You can't do that with paper files."[3]

Finding a Balance

According to Giovanni Vigna, one of the leaders of the Computer Security Group at the University of California–Santa Barbara, the challenge is to find the appropriate balance between digital technology's ease of use and security. In his view, building computer systems that are 100 percent secure is too cumbersome and not feasible. "Think about 17 locks on your car," he says. "Would you buy a car like that?"[4]

In addition, Vigna says that the majority of users are not computer savvy enough to protect themselves adequately online. Often this leads to mistakes that expose users' vulnerabilities. While physical theft is easily discovered, cybertheft can be much more difficult to discover. In fact, many users may not understand computer systems enough to recognize they have been hacked by a cybercriminal until weeks or months after the crime. "We need to find metaphors so people can understand computer security as well as they understand physical security," said Vigna. He describes cybercriminals like thieves who randomly twist doorknobs, looking for one that is unlocked. "If you make one little mistake, you're completely opening your door to the entire world. Everyone in the world can twist your doorknob."[5]

> "We need to find metaphors so people can understand computer security as well as they understand physical security."[5]
>
> — Giovanni Vigna, one of the leaders of the Computer Security Group at the University of California–Santa Barbara.

Chapter One

Going Online: A Growing Risk

In 2009 an employee at the National Archives and Records Administration (NARA) sent a defective computer hard drive to a vendor for repair. When the vendor determined that the drive could not be fixed, it passed the drive to another firm for recycling. The drive that passed unsecured from company to company contained detailed personal information, including Social Security numbers for as many as 70 million US veterans.

Hank Bellomy, a NARA IT manager, reported the incident to NARA's inspector general. Bellomy believes that NARA's practice of returning hard drives to vendors without cleaning them of information is irresponsible. "This is the single largest release of personally identifiable information by the government ever. . . . We leaked 70 million records, and no one has heard a word of it," he said in an interview. Bellomy added that he is worried about the potential consequences of NARA's past handling of online data. "We have no clue how many drives have been sent back over the past seven years since this system was in place,"[6] he said.

Revolutionizing Lives

Digital technology and the Internet have become a powerful influence in many people's lives. According to a report by the Pew Internet & American Life Project, 93 percent of American teens between the ages of 12 and 17 and 74 percent of adults went online as of September 2009.

The Internet has become a place for users to find information, shop, and pay bills. Instead of driving to the mall to browse through retail stores, people can shop online stores from their homes. According to the Pew report, nearly half (48 percent) of online teens use the Internet to buy things like books, clothing, or music. Adults are even more likely to shop online, with 75 percent reporting that they have purchased items online.

In addition, a *Generations Online 2010* report by the Pew Internet & American Life Project found that some key online activities have become universally popular across all age groups. These include e-mail, using search engines, researching health information, reading news, shopping, online banking, and making online charitable donations.

In the case of online banking, people are no longer limited by a traditional bank's hours and locations. They can pay bills, transfer money between accounts, and buy and sell investments whenever they want from the comfort of their home computers. This convenience has transformed online banking into one of the fastest-growing Internet activities. According to a 2009 survey by the Gartner Group, 47 percent of Americans reported that they bank online. "It's pretty hard not to do online banking because it is so convenient, and people want convenience,"[7] says Atul Prakash, a University of Michigan researcher who conducted a study on the risks of Internet banking.

> **"Surpassing one billion global users is a significant landmark in the history of the Internet. It is a monument to the increasingly unified global community in which we live."[8]**
>
> — Magid Abraham, president and chief executive officer of comScore, an Internet marketing research company.

Evolution of the Internet

The Internet was originally designed for the US military as a way for computers to share information over long distances. In 1969 the military funded a research network then named Arpanet. It connected the computers at five sites and allowed them to "talk" to each other. This system of communication eventually evolved into the Internet. As it grew, it connected millions of computers around the globe and formed a communication network.

In the 1980s people communicated in small groups through closed networks on the Internet. Telephone lines and modems physically connected computers to the Internet. However, using the Internet was not simple. Websites or web pages did not exist. Data sharing was not user-friendly. Without a technical background, information was difficult to find. In fact, the early Internet was used primarily by computer experts, engineers, scientists, and librarians. There were very few home or office personal computers. Anyone who used the Internet had to learn a very complicated system.

In addition, because the Internet was funded by the government initially, it was limited to research, education, and government uses. Commercial uses were prohibited. This policy changed in the 1990s with the development of independent commercial networks. They made it possible for commercial websites to route traffic from site to site without using the government-funded network.

The World Wide Web

The introduction of the World Wide Web in 1991 also made using the Internet much easier for the average person. The web was a new system to create, organize, and link documents and web pages so that people could easily read them over the Internet. If the Internet was a system of networks that connected people, the World Wide Web was the means for people to use that connectivity.

The creation of the web browser further simplified Internet use. Browser software communicated with the Internet. It translated web pages and data into an easy-to-read format on computer screens. Browsers such as Netscape and Internet Explorer helped people of all ages and backgrounds use the Internet.

With the invention of the World Wide Web and web browsers, the Internet grew at a rapid pace. The number of computers connected to the Internet has grown from a few computer scientists in the late 1960s to 1.5 billion consumers worldwide today. It has also become a global phenomenon, with some of the fastest growth found in Asia and Europe. Magid Abraham, president and chief executive officer of comScore, an Internet marketing research company, says:

> Surpassing one billion global users is a significant landmark in the history of the Internet. It is a monument to the increasingly unified

global community in which we live. . . . The second billion will be online before we know it, and the third billion will arrive even faster than that, until we have a truly global network of interconnected people and ideas that transcend borders and cultural boundaries.[8]

Web Use Changes

As more people became connected to the Internet, the ways in which they used it began to change. At first people used the Internet passively. They read information but did little to add to it or change what they found online. Around 2002 this pattern of use began to change. People started using the Internet more interactively. They could post writing, pictures, video, and music on the web. They invited others to view and comment on their sites. They were no longer just absorbing the information in front of them. Instead they were creating and adding their own information.

Research, banking, and shopping are among the most popular online activities across all age groups, with health information being a common subject for online searches. A free medical app (pictured) benefits physicians while laypeople have many other online choices for finding similar information.

Around the same time, e-commerce exploded on the Internet. Introduced in the mid-1990s, e-commerce is the buying and selling of products or services over the Internet. According to a 2010 report by investment firm J.P. Morgan, global e-commerce was predicted to reach $680 billion in 2011.

Although digital technology and the Internet have transformed lives with convenience and ability to connect people around the globe, they have also introduced new security concerns. When confidential data was physically stored on paper, thieves could only steal as much as they could carry. Today sensitive data is recorded electronically and stored on computer hard drives, disks, and networks. While it is more convenient for users, electronically stored data is also more vulnerable to accidental disclosure or theft. Thousands and sometimes even millions of records can be transmitted or downloaded and stolen in just a few minutes.

Online Security Concerns Grow

Americans are increasingly becoming concerned about online security. According to Mintel, a market research firm, a 2008 survey found that 65 percent of adults were more concerned about online security than they were five years earlier. "Identity theft and online security are hot issues in the media, making them top-of-mind for consumers," says Susan Menke, a senior analyst at Mintel. "More people now realize the harmful effects of identity theft, so they're growing increasingly wary of doing business online or responding to unsolicited emails."[9]

> "More people now realize the harmful effects of identity theft, so they're growing increasingly wary of doing business online or responding to unsolicited emails."[9]
>
> — Susan Menke, a senior analyst at Mintel.

Online security is also a growing concern for companies. In 2010 Symantec conducted a global survey of 2,152 small to medium-sized businesses. In the survey, businesses ranked online attacks and information loss as their top business risks.

In addition to external risks from hackers, companies face internal security risks from employees. A 2010 Trend Micro study of 1,600 workers in the United States, United Kingdom, Germany, and Japan revealed

Automated Billing and Online Security

Many consumers sign up for automatic billing plans to pay recurring charges. These are convenient and hassle free, and consumers never have to remember to pay their bills. Instead the company automatically charges their credit cards or bank accounts each month. Yet despite the convenience, automatic billing plans can be an online security risk when unscrupulous employees access and steal private information.

In April 2011 the online movie company Netflix informed the New Hampshire Attorney General's office that a company employee had accessed an undisclosed number of customer names and credit card numbers without authorization. Upon learning of the data breach, Netflix fired the employee and notified the attorney general. They also notified customers whose data had been taken. According to company spokesperson Steve Swasey, Netflix takes safeguarding customer personal data and privacy seriously and deals swiftly with any issues as they arise.

that many employees are careless with company data. Approximately 50 percent admitted to sending sensitive corporate data over unsecured web mail accounts. "These results might be disturbing to IT administrators and small business owners, but they're not all that surprising, especially to those of us who work within the security industry,"[10] says David Perry, Trend Micro's global director of education.

Government agencies also say that online security is one of the biggest challenges facing chief information officers (CIOs) of federal agencies. A survey conducted by TechAmerica, a technology trade association, showed that federal CIOs say that external threats to their IT networks are rising. Several reported that their agencies see millions of malicious hacking attempts daily. "This is forcing agencies to change how they think about cyber security and to establish security controls,"[11] says Alma Cole, director of information for Customs and Border Protection's security operations center.

How Online Security Breaches Occur

Data breaches on home computers, company networks, or government servers can occur in several ways. One of the most common reasons for online data breaches is human error. Errors occur when an employee mistakenly sends an e-mail with confidential information to the wrong e-mail address or an entire distribution list. In some cases employees have lost or misplaced laptops and hard drives that hold personal information. In one example of human error, an employee at the Washington, DC, Office of the State Superintendent of Education mistakenly e-mailed personal data for 2,400 students to more than 1,000 people. The leaked data included information such as names, e-mail and home addresses, phone and Social Security numbers, and dates of birth. Some people expressed anger over the mix-up. "We tell [our daughter] how important it is not to give her Social Security number out, not even to join Facebook, for goodness sakes,"[12] said Brenda Thomas, the mother of a student whose information was leaked.

In other cases data breaches occur when a security lapse allows a user to download documents or delete or change data without authorization.

> "The United States' reliance on the Internet and dependence on automated systems connected to it represent a massive vulnerability."[14]
>
> — Robert Knake, cybersecurity expert at the Council on Foreign Relations, a nonprofit think tank.

In 2010 hundreds of thousands of sensitive and classified US military and government documents were leaked to WikiLeaks, an online antisecrecy group. WikiLeaks published several thousand of these classified documents on its website for the world to read. Army private Bradley Manning was charged with illegally downloading the documents from government servers and providing them to WikiLeaks. US officials said that Manning's actions put many lives at risk by revealing the identities of people secretly working with the United States and potentially jeopardized the country's relationships with other nations.

Sometimes data breaches occur when a cybercriminal hacks into computer systems and steals sensitive data. In 2009 Heartland Payment Systems, a payment processing company, announced that hackers had broken into its computer systems. Hackers gained access to Heartland's system, which processed about 100 million credit card transactions per month for 175,000 merchants. Police investigating the crime arrested 3 men in 2009 who were part of an international stolen credit card ring. The men had used the stolen Heartland data to create electronic Visa gift cards, which they used to purchase goods from stores and later sold for cash.

Consequences of Data Breaches

If sensitive information falls into the wrong hands after a data breach, the consequences can be far-reaching. For individuals, data breaches can lead to identity theft. Since 2005 more than 240 million records containing sensitive personal data have been exposed in data breaches. While not every data breach leads to identity theft, the costs of those that do is estimated at more than $50 billion annually. In addition, it can take months or years for identity theft victims to restore their credit and damaged reputations. If hackers infect computers with malware during a data breach, it can cost thousands of dollars to replace or repair infected computers and systems. Malware is malicious software designed to damage or disrupt a computer or network.

After a corporate data breach, companies incur significant costs in term of time and money to restore and repair systems and notify customers whose information may have been leaked. In April 2011 hackers breached Sony Corporation's online entertainment networks. They may have stolen personal information that could expose as many as 100 million Sony customers to years of potential identity theft. Michael Pachter, an analyst with Wedbush Securities, estimates that Sony's costs resulting from the breach will reach $50 million. In addition, Sony will have to win back the confidence of customers. Lawrence Ponemon, founder of the Ponemon Institute, estimated it would take Sony about 6 months to stabilize sales and consumer confidence. "During that period, a company like Sony can lose millions of dollars,"[13] he said.

> "The weakest link is still people. As good as IT measures and technologies can be, the biggest problems occur wherever technology comes into contact with people who need to administer, manage or even use IT security functionality."[15]
>
> — Sachar Paulus, former chief security officer of German software company SAP AG.

For governments, the leak of classified information can lead to vulnerabilities in telecommunications, military operations, and water supply and power distribution networks. In the wrong hands this information could provide a roadmap for terrorists to attack a country's systems and infrastructure. According to a 2008 US Government Accountability Office (GAO) report, the Tennessee Valley Authority, the country's largest public power company, is vulnerable to cyberattacks. If attacked, critical systems that provide electricity to more than 8.7 million people could fail. The GAO report found that the power company's corporate network, which is connected to the Internet, is also linked to systems that control power production. Cyberattackers could penetrate security weaknesses in the corporate network and gain control of or destroy the power systems. "The United States' reliance on the Internet and depen-

WikiLeaks published several thousand classified documents online in 2010 and again in 2011. In a massive breach of security, the documents were illegally downloaded and passed on to the antisecrecy group by a US Army private.

Organized Cybercrime

Just a few years ago, most hackers worked alone. Individual hackers sent phishing e-mails (which try to trick users into revealing personal information), built phony websites, and profited from the resulting fraud. Because large amounts of money can be made in online scams, law enforcement warns that cybercrime has become more sophisticated than ever. Gangs of organized criminals are banding together to steal users' money. Working in teams, the criminals can specialize, with each member focusing on one piece of the gang's operations. Coders or techies maintain the infrastructure such as servers and Internet service providers, while hackers probe for application and network vulnerabilities to attack. Fraudsters create phishing and spam schemes, and money mules execute wire or bank transfers to move stolen money for the gang.

According to David Perry, global director of education for Trend Micro, an antivirus software company, organized cybercrime is a billion-dollar business around the world. In one example, he said that US law enforcement busted a Ukrainian cybergang that made $900 million in one month.

dence on automated systems connected to it represent a massive vulnerability,"[14] said Robert Knake, a cybersecurity expert at the Council on Foreign Relations, a nonprofit think tank.

Defenses Down

Even though the risks and consequences of an online data breach are high, many people, companies, and governments are not fully protecting their online information. According to the *Consumer Reports* 2007 State of the Net survey, 17 percent of computer owners do not have antivirus software installed, a key component in blocking unwanted attacks on personal data. Thirty-three percent do not use spyware blocking to prevent identity theft. In addition, 3.7 million households with broadband

Internet access have not installed a firewall to protect their computers and electronic files.

Companies and governments are not faring much better. As of 2010 the Department of Homeland Security reports that two-thirds of federal agencies are not continuously monitoring their networks and 8 percent had no monitoring systems in place at all. Many corporations are jumping into the latest technologies and procedures, such as smartphones and cloud computing, without first analyzing the security implications.

With the digital technology landscape rapidly evolving, companies and governments are often unprepared and scrambling to keep up with security for the latest hardware, software, and procedures. Yet even when they employ the most up-to-date defenses, users who circumvent security procedures may be exposing an organization's online data to potential breaches. Sachar Paulus, former chief security officer of German software company SAP AG, explains:

> The weakest link is still people. As good as IT measures and technologies can be, the biggest problems occur wherever technology comes into contact with people who need to administer, manage or even use IT security functionality. One of the best examples is related to protecting confidential information over the Internet using e-mail encryption. Existing tools are still too cumbersome for people to actually use it the right way. Many people use encryption but then send the password for the encryption in the same e-mail, so what's the use?[15]

As Internet use evolves, keeping up with rapid technological change is a challenging but necessary step to secure the online world. New digital technology creates vulnerabilities for individuals, companies, and governments, and hackers are constantly looking for ways to exploit those vulnerabilities.

Chapter Two

Identity Theft

In February 2009 Dave Crouse began noticing several small but suspicious charges on his bank statement—and then suddenly the charges began increasing. Even when he closed the bank account and opened a new one at a different bank, fraudulent charges showed up again. Over a 6-month period, approximately $900,000 was charged to Crouse's debit card and bank account. Cyberthieves had stolen Crouse's online identity and opened multiple credit cards and bank accounts in his name. As a result, Crouse's credit history has been destroyed. In addition, his attempts to clear his name and financial records have cost him nearly $100,000. "My identity is public knowledge and even though it's ruined, they're still using it. . . . It ruined me financially and emotionally,"[16] says Crouse.

Before the identify theft, Crouse frequently shopped online, using his bank debit card to pay for purchases. He suspects that his computer was infected by keystroke malware, a malicious program that records everything a user types, and that this malware was used to steal his personal information. A cyberthief had probably hacked into one of the websites Crouse regularly shopped, and his computer got infected. The malware recorded all of Crouse's personal information as he unknowingly typed and delivered it to the cyberthieves. With information such as Crouse's Social Security number, address, and phone number, cyberthieves could open multiple credit cards in his name and link them to his bank accounts.

Identity theft affected Crouse's life in many ways. He fell behind on paying bills and incurred mounting late fees, interest expenses, and penalties. Unemployed, the financial mess even hurt his job search. One recruiter told him that companies turned him away because his credit reports were so bad and his debt was too high. "It affected me. It affected my livelihood. It affected my whole family,"[17] says Crouse.

What Is Identity Theft?

Identity theft like what Crouse experienced occurs when personal information is stolen and used for another person's gain. It can be as simple as credit card theft or as complicated as a thief assuming a victim's complete identity. While identity theft existed long before computers and the Internet, the recent increase in online shopping and banking has made identity theft a growing concern. Chris E. McGoey, a professional security consultant based near Los Angeles, says: "Identity theft has always been with us—forever. The Internet is making it grow at an exponential level. There are all kinds of scams out there. Now it's just easier."[18]

Experts say that thieves have devised many methods for getting the information they need. Sometimes thieves steal addresses and phone

When a computer is infected by spyware or other types of malicious software the result can be devastating. This Michigan business owner lost two days of computer time because of spyware that prevented him from processing payroll deductions and accessing contractor bids.

numbers of potential victims and then go to the Internet to find matching Social Security numbers. In other cases they construct phony websites that trick unsuspecting victims into entering personal information.

Other times cyberthieves use malicious software called malware that infects a user's computer. Malware can be attached to an e-mail message or picked up from an infected website. When the user opens the file or clicks on an infected link, malware downloads onto the user's computer without his or her knowledge. One type of malware, called spyware, tracks every keystroke made on the computer, such as online passwords, Social Security numbers, and account numbers. Often, users never know that their every stroke is being recorded. The spyware then sends the stolen information to cyberthieves.

With a user's personal information, online identity thieves can get addresses changed on the victim's existing bank or credit card accounts. Alternatively, they can open new accounts in the victim's name. Thieves can charge purchases, withdraw money from users' bank accounts, and assume users' identities online.

> "Identity theft has always been with us—forever. The Internet is making it grow at an exponential level. There are all kinds of scams out there. Now it's just easier."[18]
>
> — Chris E. McGoey, a professional security consultant based near Los Angeles.

Risk of Identity Theft

Anyone who goes online is at risk for identity theft. According to a report by Javelin Strategy & Research, a market research and consulting company, 8.1 million adults in the United States were victims of identity theft in 2010. People who spend the most money and use the Internet for shopping and banking are the most vulnerable. "The more you transact, the more you're at risk because you leave a trail behind,"[19] says James Van Dyke, Javelin president and founder. Young adults aged 18 to 24 also have a higher risk of being identity theft victims because they simply do not pay enough attention to their accounts or protect themselves online.

Consumers are also at risk of identity theft when companies and government agencies store their personal information electronically. Some of the largest online data breaches occur within companies or governmental agencies. "Companies we deal with daily have all of our sensitive information in mega databases, which are vulnerable to unscrupulous

What Your Hard Drive Tells Identity Thieves

With technology changing so quickly, many people upgrade their computers every few years. In the process they erase sensitive and personal data from the hard drive, then turn the computer in for recycling or sell it on eBay. What they do not realize is that simply erasing data from a hard drive may not permanently remove it. Instead, with simple and inexpensive software, anyone can restore the files and access the user's personal information.

Users may not be aware that they are exposing their personal information to unknown viewers. To demonstrate the danger, researchers from *Consumer Reports* bought several hard drives on eBay that the sellers described as reformatted or wiped clean. The researchers used a simple software program and successfully restored many deleted files. Some of the information they recovered included tax documents, MySpace account names and passwords, e-mails, photographs, and favorite website lists. Simson Garfinkel, a research fellow at Harvard University, reports a similar result in his research. Of the more than 1,200 hard drives that he has examined, Garfinkel estimates that only one-third to one-half were properly cleaned.

employees and hackers,"[20] says Mari Frank, an attorney and identity theft victim. In these cases millions of people can be exposed to identity theft in a single incident. For example, a Salina, Kansas, hospital alerted 1,100 patients in 2007 when a laptop containing their names, Social Security numbers, and medical histories was stolen. Thieves also stole a government computer that included names, Social Security numbers, and birth dates of more than 26 million US veterans in 2006. In each case the affected individuals are at risk that criminals will use their stolen personal information for identity theft.

Cost of Identity Theft

If online thieves use personal information to charge purchases or empty bank accounts, the cost of recovery can be significant. Although many banks and credit card companies will reimburse charges if a victim can prove his or her identity was stolen, the average victim spends $631 per incident in out-of-pocket costs. These costs include paying off fraudulent charges, late fees, and legal costs.

In addition to out-of-pocket costs, some victims of identity theft spend months, even years, trying to clear their names. Debra Guenterberg and her husband have been battling identity theft since 1996. Someone—the Guenterbergs do not know whom—stole the couple's Social Security numbers and then opened credit cards and bought cars and three homes using their names. To restore their credit, the Guenterbergs have worked with the IRS, elected officials, and local sheriffs. Despite their efforts, they were turned down for credit in 2009 because of the damage identity theft has done to their financial records. "It's a nightmare. We both feel physically and mentally exhausted. We feel hopeless because we can't fix this,"[21] says Debra.

Financial Identity Theft

There are several types of identity theft, and each one affects victims differently. One of the most common is financial identity theft. Thieves steal personal information and use a victim's existing credit cards to purchase merchandise or empty a bank account. Other times, cyberthieves will use stolen data to open credit cards and bank accounts in the victim's name. Then they embark on a spending spree, leaving the victim with the bills. Sometimes identity thieves will combine stolen personal information from several victims. Called synthetic identity theft, this process creates a new identity from the pieces of each victim's information.

> "Companies we deal with daily have all of our sensitive information in mega databases, which are vulnerable to unscrupulous employees and hackers."[20]
>
> — Mari Frank, an attorney and identity theft victim.

Children are a vulnerable target for financial identity thieves. From the moment a baby is born and assigned a Social Security number, identity thieves can steal his or her information to use in criminal activities. Because most parents do not think about looking at a credit report for their kids, thieves can get away with using a child's identity for years.

Heavy users of online banking and shopping are more vulnerable to identify theft than those who use such services less often. Young adults are at greatest risk because they tend to pay less attention to their online accounts than older people.

According to the Identity Theft Resource Center, a nonprofit identity theft support and education organization, nearly 10 percent of its cases during the last six months of 2009 involved child identity theft.

Many parents may not realize that seemingly harmless online activities are exposing their children to financial identity theft. Like many moms, Lauren DeArmas posts her baby daughter's pictures on Facebook. "It doesn't cross your mind about that, taking an infant's identity, what can you do with that?"[22] DeArmas says. But experts warn that identity thieves can get a child's identity with simple information such as name, birth date, and birth city—details that are often posted online by parents. "Right away you have a name of the baby and you have a date of birth of the baby, now from that they can take and create an identity if they want,"[23] says Florida state attorney Katherine Fernandez-Rundle.

Medical Identity Theft

Thieves can also use stolen personal information to steal a victim's medical identity. Sometimes a thief will use a victim's name and Social Security number to receive emergency room treatment. In other cases thieves steal basic health insurance information such as the member ID and group policy numbers on a medical card. With this information, the thief can pretend to be the victim and receive any type of medical care, from doctor's visits to surgery. Even more commonly, thieves who work in hospitals or medical offices download personal insurance data from computers, then use it to make fraudulent insurance company billings or sell it on the black market.

Brandon Sharp learned he was a victim of medical identity theft when he applied for a mortgage in 2003. After receiving his credit report, he was shocked to discover that he had thousands of dollars of debt for emergency room visits around the county. "There was even a $19,000 bill for a Life Flight air ambulance service in some remote location I'd never heard of. I had emergency room bills from places like Bowling Green, Kan., where I've never even visited. I'm still cleaning up the mess,"[24] says Sharp.

Like Sharp, many people do not know for months or even years that their medical identities have been stolen. During that time, insurance companies may pay the fraudulent bills. Often victims do not discover the theft until they file their own medical claims. Then the insurance company may notify them that they have already reached the insurance policy's lifetime benefit limit. Alternately, victims may notice errors in their medical files during a doctor or hospital visit. These discrepancies arise because a thief has been using their medical identity. The errors could be life-threatening when critical information like blood type or allergies is listed incorrectly.

> "Once you aggregate and put data in one place, it's easier for you to see it, but it's also easier for a criminal to see and use it. The digitization of medical records over the next years is certainly going to make this more of an issue."[25]
>
> — Scott Mitic, chief executive of TrustedID, a consumer data–protection firm.

Because medical identity theft takes so long to detect, it is approximately two and a half times more costly than other types of identity theft, according to Van Dyke, president of Javelin Strategy & Research.

In 2009 the average cost of medical identity theft was approximately $12,100, as compared with $4,841 for other types of identity theft.

According to Javelin Strategy & Research, there were more than 275,000 cases of medical information theft in 2009. Privacy experts are concerned that those numbers will increase dramatically as more health records move online. Scott Mitic, chief executive of TrustedID, a consumer data–protection firm, says: "Once you aggregate and put data in one place, it's easier for you to see it, but it's also easier for a criminal to see and use it. The digitization of medical records over the next years is certainly going to make this more of an issue."[25]

Criminal Identity Theft

Criminal identity theft occurs when a person gives another person's name and personal information to police during an investigation or arrest. Often the imposter will have a fake driver's license or other type of identification in the victim's name. Victims often know nothing about the identity fraud until they are stopped for a routine traffic violation and police arrest them because of an outstanding warrant. Other times, victims apply for jobs but fail the employer background checks because of a false criminal history found under their name. According to a survey of identity theft victims conducted by the Identity Theft Resource Center in 2009, 32 percent of respondents said that identity thieves had pretended to be the victim and gave the victim's identity information to police when arrested for a crime. In addition, 23 percent reported that criminals were convicted of crimes while using the victim's identity, resulting in a criminal record for the victim.

> "Unfortunately, the hackers are always one step ahead, and it doesn't mean that the company has done anything wrong. Sometimes, it's impossible to be 100 percent secure."[29]
>
> — Kristen J. Mathews, a partner at a New York law firm and head of its privacy and data security group.

When Jeff Goldsmith of Elkhart, Indiana, saw the police at his house in 2009, he thought they were looking for his neighbors. Instead the police handcuffed Goldsmith and arrested him for allegedly beating his girlfriend's son in Fort Wayne, Indiana. Yet Goldsmith did not have a girlfriend. He had been happily married for 20 years. And he had not been to Fort Wayne since he took his grandchildren to the zoo in 2007.

When the police investigated Goldsmith's claims of innocence, they discovered that he was the victim of criminal identity theft. When the warrant had been issued for the real suspect, the police had all of Goldsmith's identifying information, including name and Social Security

Fake driver's licenses (such as the ones displayed here) can be made with information stolen from personal computers and some e-mail and web transactions. Often victims have no idea that their personal information has been stolen until they apply for a job or are stopped for a traffic violation.

number. Only the physical description was different. Goldsmith says that he had an early indication that his identity had been stolen when he received two bills—one for car insurance on a truck he did not own and another for a phone bill in Arkansas. After he cleared the bills from his name, Goldsmith monitored his credit report and believed that the matter was over. Because police still have not caught the real suspect, Goldsmith says he plans to apply for a new Social Security number to prevent any more mix-ups.

Fighting Identity Theft

Regardless of the form it takes, identity theft can have serious consequences for victims. To protect citizens, many states have enacted laws against cybercriminals and identity theft. Some states restrict the use of Social Security numbers as identifiers in public and private documents. In addition, a majority of states require companies who have been hacked to notify the people whose personal information may have been stolen. "The law applies to businesses and state government agencies that maintain databases when there is a breach involving the acquisition of information such as Social Security numbers, credit card numbers, drivers licenses, and other vulnerable personal information,"[26] says Democratic New York State Assembly member James Brennan.

In addition, the federal government has passed several laws to protect consumers from cybercriminals. In 1998 Congress passed the Identity Theft and Assumption Deterrence Act, which makes knowingly using another person's identification for any unlawful activity a felony. The Fair and Accurate Credit Transactions Act of 2003 establishes requirements for consumer reporting agencies, creditors, and others to help remedy identity theft. The act gives victims of identity theft certain rights and privileges to recover losses from the crime, including free access to credit reports and blocking information related to identity theft on credit reports.

In 2004 Congress passed the Identity Theft Penalty Enhancement Act, which made prison sentences harsher for those convicted of identity theft. The act added two years in prison for anyone convicted of using stolen personal information to pose as another person. It added an additional five years in prison for those who use stolen personal informa-

Phishing for Personal Information

Phishing begins with an e-mail, instant message, or pop-up message. The message looks like it comes from a user's bank, Internet service provider, credit card company, or retailer. The message usually instructs a user to take immediate action in order to avoid a negative consequence such as a bank account being closed. It might direct the user to log on to a bogus website or call a phone number where they will be asked to verify personal information such as Social Security numbers, credit card numbers, or bank accounts and passwords. Sometimes phishing e-mails contain an attached file that launches malicious software, or malware, when opened. The malware may record keystrokes or data such as e-mail addresses and send the information to the thief. Sometimes malware allows the thief to control the victim's computer remotely for a future attack.

Regardless of how the phishing attacks occur, the end result is that cyberthieves gain access to information that allows them to steal money, identities, or both. Investigators report that phishing scams typically yield a positive response rate of 1 to 5 percent. With scammers being able to send out hundreds of thousands of phishing messages in a few minutes, millions of people have fallen for the scams.

tion for terrorism. The act could help prosecutors go after cybergangs that work together to commit online crime. "These are networks and often you only have one small tentacle of it in [a] courtroom," says Jim Vaules, vice president and fraud expert at archival firm LexisNexis. "If [prosecutors] have a tool that changes the sentencing guidelines from probation to a prison sentence, it could have significant results in people cooperating with the government and exposing larger parts of the criminal network."[27]

In 2008 President George W. Bush signed the Identity Theft Enforcement and Restitution Act into law. Previously, prosecutors needed to show that hackers and cybercriminals had caused a minimum of $5,000 in damage before they could prosecute a case. The 2008 act eliminated that requirement, making it easier for identity theft victims to win compensation for their financial losses and time spent fixing their damaged credit and accounts.

Investigation Challenges

Investigating and prosecuting identity theft can be challenging for even the most experienced law enforcement officers. There are no witnesses, crime scenes, or fingerprints. Instead cybercriminals work in obscurity; they might even be thousands of miles away from their victims. In fact, most identity theft occurs across jurisdictional borders, making it difficult for different agencies to coordinate investigating a crime.

Sometimes the lack of cooperation from entities affected by identity theft is a challenge for investigators. Victims include users, banks and credit card companies that reimburse fraudulent charges, and companies whose corporate networks have been breached. Coordinating and gaining the cooperation of all victims can sometimes be difficult for investigators. Some individuals or companies may not want to allow law enforcement officers access to personal and financial records needed to investigate the crime. Because of these challenges, law enforcement officers report that few identity theft cases are actually solved.

Identity Theft Task Force

To help investigators, President George W. Bush established the President's Task Force on Identity Theft in 2006. Chaired by the attorney general and cochaired by the chair of the Federal Trade Commission (FTC), the task force works to coordinate federal, state, and local law enforcement efforts. In 2007 the task force also issued a national strategic plan to combat identity theft. The plan addressed ways to improve effective prosecutions of identity theft and better data protection for sensitive personal information stored by companies, businesses, government agencies, and citizens. "Identity theft is a crime that goes far beyond the loss of money or property," said Attorney General Alberto Gonzales when announcing the plan's completion. "It is a personal invasion, done in secret that can rob innocent men and women of their good names. The strategic plan we are releasing today is part of a comprehensive effort to fight this crime, protect consumers, and help victims put their lives back together."[28]

Data Insecurity

The Internet and the digital age have transformed the way people communicate, do business, and find information. Yet with so much information moving online, data security and the resulting risk of identity theft are a serious concern. Without realizing their mistakes, users may be exposing themselves to an online security breach.

Even when Internet users are diligent about online security, they can be vulnerable when companies and government agencies put sensitive data online. Although companies use the latest technology and procedures to protect data, persistent hackers frequently find a way to get in. "Unfortunately, the hackers are always one step ahead, and it doesn't mean that the company has done anything wrong," says Kristen J. Mathews, a partner at a New York law firm and head of its privacy and data security group. "Sometimes, it's impossible to be 100 percent secure."[29]

Chapter Three

Securing Company Networks

In January 2010 Google executives announced that the company had been the target of a sophisticated and coordinated cyberattack against its corporate network. Hackers stole company secrets and attempted to access the Gmail accounts of Chinese human rights activists. According to Google, the attack originated in China with an instant message sent to a Google employee based in that country. When the employee clicked on a link in the message, it connected him to a corrupted website, which allowed hackers to access his computer. From there the hackers were able to access the computers of Google software developers in California and gain control of a software repository used by the Google development team. The hackers were also able to breach Google's password system that controls access for millions of users of the company's web services.

In the attack, the hackers used almost a dozen pieces of malware and several levels of encryption to reach into the corporate network and hide their tracks. "The encryption was highly successful in obfuscating [hiding] the attack and avoiding common detection methods. We haven't seen encryption at this level. It was highly sophisticated,"[30] says Dmitri Alperovitch, vice president of threat research for McAfee, an Internet security company.

Because Google learned of the security breach shortly after it happened, it was able to respond quickly and make significant changes to its network security. Yet the fact that the hackers were able to access a critical software repository opens the risk that they may have found corporate network weaknesses that Google executives do not know about. "It's obviously a real issue if you can understand how the system works. Understanding the algorithms on which the software is based might be of great value to an attacker looking for weak points in the system,"[31] says Rodney Joffe, a vice president at Neustar, a developer of Internet infrastructure services. And because Google holds the personal information of millions of customers and individuals, each may be at risk of having their personal data stolen and used for criminal activity.

Corporate Security Threats

Companies like Google that store customer or corporate data online or in electronic databases are vulnerable to data breaches that release that information to unintended parties. Beyond customer data, valuable company information such as product designs, business plans, patents,

The web giant Google has experienced several security breaches as a result of coordinated cyberattacks. One such attack took place in early 2010; another occurred in mid-2011. In both instances, Google traced the origins of the attack to hackers in China.

Zero-Day Attacks

Even with the most up-to-date security software, computers may still be at risk because of unknown vulnerabilities in operating systems or software applications. A zero-day attack is a virus or other action that takes advantage of these vulnerabilities before the software developer has had time to create a fix or patch for the problem. Microsoft products such as Internet Explorer, Office, and the Windows operating system have been common targets of zero-day attacks, partially because so many people use them.

Software companies typically use tools to help them find flaws in their own products before anyone else does. When they do, they develop a security patch, then announce the flaw and distribute the patch to users and company IT staff. The intent is for users to install the patch and plug the vulnerability before hackers can exploit the vulnerability. Yet at the same time, hackers are also probing and testing popular software applications, looking for a vulnerability from which they can profit. If they find one, they can launch their own attack or sell the information on the black market to another hacker.

trademarks, and financial information are all at risk of falling into the wrong hands when a security breach occurs.

In many cases employee error causes an online security breach. In 2010 an employee for the Entertainment Software Rating Board mistakenly hit "reply all" on an e-mail, sending 1,000 customer e-mail addresses to an unauthorized distribution list. At the University of South Carolina, human error caused the leak of personal information, including Social Security numbers, of approximately 31,000 people in 2010. At Missouri State University in 2010, an employee was supposed to upload a list that contained the names and Social Security numbers of more than 6,000 students to a secure server accessible only to university employees. Instead the employee mistakenly uploaded the data to an insecure server. There it was exposed to Google spiders, special software robots used by search engines to save information found on websites in searchable databases. The spiders indexed the information on the web for anyone to read.

Even the best-trained employees can make mistakes. In fact, employee error is the leading cause of online data breaches. According to a 2010 data breach report from the Ponemon Institute, nearly 41 percent of data breaches in 2010 were caused by employee negligence. "Securing information continues to challenge organizations at all levels, but the vast majority of these breaches are preventable," says Francis deSouza, senior vice president of Symantec's Enterprise Security Group. He recommends that companies create a "culture of security"[32] that includes training, data security policy, and technology.

In other cases corporate security lapses allow insiders to violate company policies and download, change, or delete sensitive information. In one case a Blue Cross Blue Shield employee who was authorized to access physician data on the company's encrypted servers violated company policy by downloading an unencrypted file to a laptop. The file contained personal information on thousands of physicians, which may have included names, Social Security numbers, and tax identification numbers. Subsequently, the laptop containing the physician data was stolen from the employee. As a result, personal information on thousands of doctors nationwide may have been exposed.

> **"Securing information continues to challenge organizations at all levels, but the vast majority of these breaches are preventable."[32]**
>
> — Francis deSouza, senior vice president of Symantec's Enterprise Security Group.

Hacking into Corporate Networks

In some cases corporate data security is breached when criminal hackers attack company networks, trying to steal company and customer information. They might use that information to commit identity theft or fraud or to conduct corporate spying. Alternately, they might sell valuable information to the highest bidder on the black market.

Hackers have developed a formidable arsenal of computer viruses, worms, and Trojan Horses—all forms of malware—that look for weaknesses in company network defenses. A virus is a computer program that spreads by infecting files or system areas of a computer or network hard drive. Then it makes copies of itself and spreads through shared discs, USB drives, or e-mail messages. While some viruses are harmless, others can damage or destroy data files. Worms can spread from computers linked on a network or the Internet. They take up valuable memory, which can cause a computer to run slowly or stop responding. Worms can also give hackers remote access to a computer. Hackers sometimes hide malicious worms and viruses in programs called Trojan horses. These pretend to do one action on a computer but instead perform a malicious action. Trojan Horses are often attached to free software downloaded from the Internet or to an e-mail message.

Malicious Attacks Increasing

Malicious attacks on corporate networks from viruses, worms, Trojan Horses, and other methods are rising in frequency. According to a 2010 data breach report from the Ponemon Institute, 31 percent of data breach cases in 2010 involved a malicious or criminal act, an increase of 7 percent over 2009. In April 2011 Sony discovered that a hacker had penetrated its online gaming and entertainment network. The thief stole names, addresses, and possibly credit card data belonging to 77 million user accounts in one of the largest-ever Internet security heists. "This is a huge data breach," says Wedbush Securities analyst Michael Pachter. "The bigger issue with Sony is how will the hacker use the info that has been illegally obtained?"[33]

After Sony learned of the break-in, the company shut down its PlayStation network immediately, but the damage might already have been done. The data breach might put millions of Sony customers worldwide at risk for identity theft for years to come. "The attackers may have your name, your birth date, potentially your mother's maiden name. These are all the things used to check your identity, and that can be used to falsify it,"[34] said Steve Ward, a spokesperson for Invincea, an online security company.

> "Data that simply leaks out of large firms—from banking to healthcare—is a bigger issue than technical hacks in many cases. Criminals simply need to know where to look."[39]
>
> — Eric Johnson, an operations management professor at Dartmouth College's Tuck School of Business.

Although Sony has not disclosed the specifics of the data breach, Alan Paller, research director of the SANS Institute, an IT training and security organization, has an idea about how it might have happened.

In one of the largest-ever Internet security heists, a hacker in 2011 stole names, addresses, and possibly credit card data belonging to 77 million Sony Corporation user accounts. The maker of the popular PlayStation game consoles shut down its network temporarily to deal with the attack.

Paller believes that it probably occurred when hackers sent an e-mail that contained a piece of malicious software to a Sony system administrator. When the employee opened the e-mail, it would have downloaded the software onto his or her computer and allowed the hackers to enter the Sony network and access the sensitive information.

Corporate Cyberspying

Sometimes other companies are the ones hacking into corporate networks. In 2010 the FBI notified executives at DuPont that hackers based in China had breached the company's computer networks for the second time in a year. Upon investigation, DuPont executives concluded that they were the target of industrial spying. Other companies, including Disney, Johnson & Johnson, and General Electric, have also been reportedly targeted by cyberspies based in China, Russia, and other countries. According to US law enforcement authorities, cyberspying on corporate networks has increased in recent years. "It appears that every industry is being victimized by [such] intrusions,"[35] said FBI deputy assistant director Steven Chabinsky.

According to a 2011 McAfee report, at least five multinational oil and gas companies have been victims of a group of hackers based in China. McAfee researchers said that the attacks appeared to be corporate espionage. The hackers broke into online oil and gas field production systems and financial documents related to field exploration and bidding on oil and gas leases. The hackers also stole information about industrial control systems. According to the report, the hackers used common hacking methods to get inside company networks. Once inside, they installed remote administration software that allowed them to control systems, search for documents, and attack other computers on the corporate network.

According to Alperovitch, McAfee's vice president for threat research, it is likely that more companies have been affected by hackers. Yet many companies are hesitant to admit that they have been hacked by cyberspies. Some fear that disclosing security breaches will generate questions from investors and regulators about the stolen information. Senator Sheldon Whitehouse of Rhode Island, who chaired a US Senate Select Committee on Intelligence task force on US cybersecurity in 2010, says: "The companies don't want to disclose it. They want to just basically eat the harm that was done to them and pretend that all is well."[36]

Economic Impact

Security breaches in corporate networks can be costly. According to the Ponemon Institute's 2010 data breach report, the cost of a data breach for a company averaged $7.2 million in 2010. Costs include data breach investigation, notification of victims, and the repair of networks, computers, and systems. In addition, companies incur costs for victim call centers, credit protection services, and lost sales and productivity. "We continue to see an increase in the costs to businesses suffering a data breach,"[37] says Larry Ponemon, chair and founder of the Ponemon Institute.

Although most any business is vulnerable to cyberattacks, companies can take steps to reduce their risk and minimize financial loss. "Companies are able to reduce the financial impact of cyber crime [by] appointing a chief information security officer (CISO), [rolling out] an enterprise security strategy and investing in technologies capable of addressing sophisticated threats,"[38] says Ponemon.

Peer-to-Peer Danger

In spite of up-to-date security on corporate networks, software introduced in the late 1990s called peer to peer (P2P) may be exposing companies to data breaches. P2P software was made popular by the music-sharing site Napster, which allowed users to share digital music files with other users who had the same software. Today P2P users can share documents, images, music, and other media files. Most P2P software is free. Anyone with a computer and an Internet connection can download it. After users install P2P software on their computer, they place files that they want to share into a special computer folder.

Although P2P is a convenient way to work or share information, it can make users vulnerable to data breaches. Many users download corrupt P2P programs or make mistakes when configuring the software. Instead of sharing a select few items, all of the files on their computer are unknowingly available to the entire P2P network.

In 2010 the FTC sent letters to nearly 100 businesses, schools, and government organizations to warn them that sensitive information about their customers and employees had been leaked through a P2P network. The leaked personal information included health data, financial records, driver's license numbers, and Social Security numbers. Eric Johnson, an operations management professor at Dartmouth College's Tuck

"As more and more of our personal information is collected and stored online and on computers, we need to ensure that the businesses storing this information are keeping it safe and giving us quick warning if it falls into the wrong hands."[45]

— Arkansas senator Mark Pryor, chair of the Subcommittee on Consumer Protection, Product Safety, and Insurance.

School of Business, says, "FTC is finally taking it seriously and warning consumers and going after firms with leaks. Data that simply leaks out of large firms—from banking to healthcare—is a bigger issue than technical hacks in many cases. Criminals simply need to know where to look."[39]

Peer-to-Peer Theft

The FTC warnings were timely, as criminals are already exploiting P2P leaks. In 2010 Jeffrey Girandola and Kajohn Phommavong were arrested for computer fraud and identity theft using P2P networks. The pair admitted that they installed P2P file-sharing software on computers. Then they searched P2P networks for account log-in information and passwords unintentionally shared by members of the networks. The men used the account information and passwords to access bank accounts and transfer money to prepaid credit cards in their own names. Then they used the prepaid credit cards to buy goods and get cash. They also redirected the online paychecks of some victims to their prepaid credit cards.

Some employees may not realize that they are putting company data at risk when they download P2P software on company-issued laptops. The employee may simply want to share music, videos, or other media files. In June 2007 a Pfizer employee installed unauthorized P2P software on a company laptop. Personal data on about 17,000 Pfizer employees was unintentionally leaked over the P2P network because it was also stored on the laptop. In a statement, FTC chair Jon Leibowitz said schools, colleges, and businesses "should take a hard look at their systems to ensure that there are no unauthorized P2P file-sharing programs and that authorized programs are properly configured and secure. Just as important, companies that distribute P2P programs, for their part, should ensure that their software design does not contribute to inadvertent file sharing."[40]

Tightening Corporate Online Security

Corporate cybercrime has become a significant problem around the world, with hackers breaching online security and stealing proprietary, sensitive business information and personal customer and employee data. A 2010 study by the Ponemon Institute concluded that cybercrime

Companies Spying on Users

In the majority of corporate online data breaches, companies are the victims. Sometimes, however, companies are the offenders, using malware to gather personal data on customers without their permission. In one case Sears Holdings Management Corporation offered customers of Sears.com and Kmart.com an invitation to sign up for My SHC Community. If the customers agreed, they would earn $10. They would also download a piece of software, which Sears said would help the company gather marketing data. Although Sears did tell the customers that it would track their online browsing, security experts said that the company did not adequately disclose the extent to which they would be tracking information. When the FTC investigated the tracking software, they found that it collected contents of shopping carts, online bank statements, medical records, and e-mail details, along with other information.

In another case customers filed a lawsuit in 2011 against Aaron's, an office supply rental chain, alleging that the company secretly spied on them. The allegations claim that Aaron's loaded spyware onto computers that it rented to customers. The spyware could then track the customers' keystrokes, make screenshots, and even take webcam images of customers using the computers in their homes or offices. According to Aaron's president, the company is taking the allegations seriously and has launched an investigation into the matter.

costs American corporations billions of dollars annually. In addition, the study found that hackers were regularly penetrating corporate network defenses. Over a four-week period, the 45 companies participating in the study experienced 50 successful attacks per week, or more than one successful attack per company each week.

In the face of these threats, companies are scrambling to fortify online security. J. Robert Beyster, chair of the Foundation for Enterprise Development, a nonprofit organization that supports entrepreneurs, says,

and on computers, we need to ensure that the businesses storing this information are keeping it safe and giving us quick warning if it falls into the wrong hands."[45]

Yet many companies are critical of data breach notification legislation. Some say that fines do more harm than good. Others argue that even when companies do everything right, they can still be breached, which may result in a fine. Mark Rasch, director of cybersecurity and privacy consulting at Computer Sciences Corporation, says, "These database breach notification laws were not intended to set standards of care. They were initially intended to help consumers, who had their information breached, to avoid identity theft. The fact is that you can do everything well, and be breached; or you can do nothing and suffer no recognizable breach."[46]

In addition, many companies oppose federal involvement in data breach notification. In 2011 a coalition of industry groups that included TechAmerica, the Center for Democracy & Technology, and the US Chamber of Commerce issued a white paper that expressed concern over potential federal cybersecurity legislation that would give the federal government authority over private sector networks. "A strong framework for promoting cyber security through a public-private partnership is already in place, and industry and government have devoted substantial resources to it," said the group. "There is no need to create a new one, or to replace the existing partnership model with a system of government mandates that would erode trust."[47] In addition, the group recommended that voluntary incentives would be more effective than fines in getting companies to invest in adequate cyberprotection.

A Significant Issue

Corporate data security has become a significant issue around the world. Employee errors are leaving corporate networks and customers exposed. Hackers are breaking into corporate networks on a regular basis, searching for confidential data that they can exploit. Yet in many cases, companies are reluctant to report breaches in online security for fear of damage to their reputations.

Recognizing these challenges, many companies large and small are investing time, money, and resources to determine the best way to defend their websites, computer networks, and other cyberassets against errors and attacks. Mary Ann Mezzapelle, a chief technologist at Hewlett Packard, says, "It comes back to one of the bottom lines about empowering the business. It means that not only do the IT people need to know more about the business, but the business needs to start taking ownership for the security of their own assets, because they are the ones that are going to have to belay the loss, whether it's data, financial, or whatever."[48]

Chapter Four

National Security and Cyberterrorism

In June 2010 a Belarus-based security company working at an Iranian nuclear power plant discovered that a computer worm called Stuxnet had infected the plant's computer systems. Cybersecurity professionals who have studied the Stuxnet worm say that it is the first known malware to attack an industrial control system like those used in power plants, gas pipelines, and dams. Some say that it is the first weaponized computer virus. "Stuxnet is really a paradigm shift as [it] is a new class and dimension of malware,"[49] said Udo Helmbrecht, executive director of the European Network and Information Security Agency.

Many believe that the Stuxnet worm was designed specifically to sabotage Iran's nuclear program, which many suspect was actively attempting to develop nuclear weapons. According to nuclear and computer experts who have studied the worm, Stuxnet appears to have included two major components. One piece sent Iran's nuclear centrifuges, which are used to create nuclear fuel, spinning out of control. At the same time, the worm sent normal readings to plant operators so that they would be unaware of the damage being created by the speeding centrifuges. In addition, a second set of codes targeted steam turbines at the Iranian plant.

At first computer experts suspected hackers or competitors launched the worm. Yet as they studied the Stuxnet code, they realized that its highly sophisticated, complex structure was the result of an enormous amount of work. They believed it was too much work, in fact, for a single entity to create. This led most to conclude that the worm was designed as a military weapon by several groups working together. "Code analysis makes it clear that Stuxnet is not about sending a message or proving a concept. It is about destroying its targets with utmost determination in military style," says Ralph Langner, an independent computer security expert in Hamburg, Germany, who studied Stuxnet. "The attackers took great care to make sure that only their designated targets were hit. It was a marksman's job."[50] Langner is concerned that the Stuxnet attack has given terrorists a blueprint for a new type of warfare, one to which many countries, including the United States, are highly vulnerable.

A worker stands at the entrance of an Iranian nuclear power plant that was the victim of a malware attack in 2010. A computer worm called Stuxnet infected the plant's computer systems in what experts described as the first-known malware attack on an industrial control system.

Threats to National Security

Cyberterrorism, such as the attacks made on Iran's nuclear systems, includes hacking into computer systems, spreading viruses, bringing websites offline, or making online threats. With the rise of the Internet and digital technology, terrorists, nations, and criminals have new tools to connect, plan, and execute attacks. Some experts believe that a well-planned cyberattack could be as devastating as a physical bomb.

In a March 2010 speech, FBI director Robert Mueller III warned that the threat of cyberterrorism was real and rapidly expanding. He said that terrorists are intent on learning hacking skills. According to Mueller, "They will either train their own recruits or hire outsiders, with an eye toward combining physical attacks with cyber attacks."[51] Although Mueller says that terrorists have not used the Internet to launch a full-scale cyberattack to date, they have defaced many websites. In 2010, hackers replaced the usual Web pages for nearly 50 members of Congress with explicit insults to President Barack Obama. No group claimed responsibility for this attack, although experts believe it might have originated in Brazil. Hackers have also executed attacks on several websites, which rendered the sites unusable for a period. While the damage has been limited in these cases, the terrorists are becoming more skilled.

According to Mueller, terror groups are using the Internet to recruit and incite terrorism. Terror group websites promote violence to a willing audience. They post videos on how to build bombs and weapons. They log on to social networking sites to share ideas and coordinate attacks. According to the Cyberterrorism Defense Analysis Center:

> The threat of cyberterrorism to our technical infrastructure is real and immediate. Computers and servers in the United States are the most aggressively targeted information systems in the world, with attacks increasing in severity, frequency, and sophistication each year. As our nation's critical infrastructure grows more reliant on information technologies, it also becomes more exposed to attackers, both foreign and domestic. These attacks can threaten our nation's economy, public works, communication systems, and computer networks.[52]

Hackers Disrupt Online Voting Test

For the November 2010 elections, the Washington, DC, elections board planned to allow some voters to send in electronic ballots over the Internet. When they tested the system in the fall, however, it was hacked after only being online for two days. A team of computer scientists from the University of Michigan hacked the website and changed the code to make it play the school's fight song.

At a DC Council committee hearing, J. Alex Halderman, a University of Michigan professor, said his team hacked the online voting system to demonstrate its security flaws. He testified that his team had gained complete control over the election board's server. He also produced almost 1,000 pages of names, addresses, and PINs for voters who had signed up to test the system. Halderman said that if it had been a real election, his team could have changed the voter's ballots. Even more concerning, his team noticed that they were not alone in the DC system. Other cyberattacks, from China and Iran, were also taking place. The DC elections board concluded that having voters submit ballots online would have to be put on hold for the foreseeable future.

Infrastructure Attacks

Cyberexperts claim terrorists could shut down parts of the Internet, phone systems, and electric grids by simply hacking into poorly defended computer systems. Years ago engineers designed the control systems for hundreds of utilities, chemical factories, air traffic control systems, and other US critical systems when each was a stand-alone entity. Now many of these utilities connect online for remote monitoring and instant communications. Without changes to older control systems, these entities are an easy target for cyberattacks.

More than 30 countries gathered in 2008 to discuss cyberterrorism and security. Among the participants was Malaysian prime minister Abdullah Ahmad Badawi, who warned that cyberattacks could trigger

Smoke billows from New York's World Trade Center after hijacked airliners slammed into the Twin Towers on September 11, 2001. US officials say that terrorist groups, like the one that carried out the 9/11 attacks, are using the Internet to recruit members and ignite terrorist sentiments.

catastrophic consequences by disrupting telecommunications networks, emergency services, financial markets, nuclear power plants, or major dams. Others point out the potential combination of physical attacks and cyberattacks. Disrupting power supply or communications during an attack could lead to greater destruction, confusion, and terror.

Stealing Classified Information

In addition to attacking infrastructure, cyberterrorists are using the Internet and digital technology to steal classified information from the United States' military and scientific institutions. Operating on the Internet from Asia and Europe, cyberthieves have penetrated networks and stolen information on satellites, rocket engines, launch systems, and the Space Shuttle.

In April 2005 cyberthieves hacked into NASA's network at the Kennedy Space Center. While workers prepared for the Space Shuttle *Discovery*'s planned launch in July, a malware program collected data from computers without detection. The program sent an unknown amount of information about the Space Shuttle to a computer system in Taiwan. According to US security experts, Taiwan is often used by the Chinese government as a digital station, leading many to suspect that the Chinese initiated the cyberattack. By December 2005 the malware had spread to a NASA satellite control complex in Maryland and to Mission Control at the Johnson Space Center in Houston. Before the malware was discovered, seven months after the initial intrusion, NASA investigators estimated that at least 30 million pages of information were gathered and sent to the Taiwan system from the Johnson Space Center.

In a 2011 report NASA's inspector general warned that NASA's network, which controls the International Space Station and the Hubble Space Telescope, remained vulnerable to attacks over the Internet. In 2009 alone, hackers stole 22 gigabytes of restricted data from the NASA Jet Propulsion Laboratory systems. Thousands of unauthorized connections from the network to systems in China, Saudi Arabia, and Estonia were also found. "Until NASA addresses these critical deficiencies and improves its IT security practices, the agency is vulnerable to computer incidents that could have a severe to catastrophic effect on agency assets, operations, and personnel,"[53] the report warned.

> "As our nation's critical infrastructure grows more reliant on information technologies, it also becomes more exposed to attackers, both foreign and domestic."[52]
>
> — Cyberterrorism Defense Analysis Center.

Bringing Down the Internet

As governments and countries increasingly rely on digital technology and the Internet for daily functioning, the Internet has become a target. By disrupting the functioning of the Internet or bringing it offline, cyberterrorists can paralyze and disrupt governments, corporations, and other organizations. Often, cyberterrorists will use a distributed denial of service attack (DDoS), in which multiple infected computers try to access targeted websites at the same time. The huge push in traffic often overwhelms the websites' servers and causes them to crash.

In 2011 hackers paralyzed the Egyptian government's websites in co-ordination with antigovernment protests. The loosely organized group of hackers from all over the world, calling themselves "Anonymous," used a DDoS attack to bring down the sites of the Ministry of Information and Egyptian president Hosni Mubarak's National Democratic Party. Anonymous has mounted several cyberattacks in the Arab world, in support of antigovernment protests, including shutting down the websites of the Tunisian government and stock exchange.

Raising Money

In addition to using the Internet to attack, spread its messages, and recruit members, terrorist organizations use the Internet to finance their activities. The Internet is a broad, efficient fund-raising tool that gives donors and the terrorist organizations anonymity in their transactions. Transferring funds through electronic payment services such as PayPal has become common. Transactions called m-payments allow people to initiate money transactions through their cell phones. In less-developed countries, using the Internet or cell phones to make money transfers is often the easiest way to initiate a transaction.

> "From now on, our digital infrastructure—the networks and computers we depend on every day—will be treated as they should be: as a strategic national asset."[55]
>
> — President Barack Obama.

According to the FBI, terrorist organizations have also used cybercrime to raise money for their activities. Younis Tsouli of Great Britain, for example, began his terrorist activity by posting videos on various websites. According to a British police investigation, he developed a relationship with the terrorist group al Qaeda in Iraq, which sent him videos to upload. When the free sites he first used became too slow for the large video files, Tsouli began to use websites with better technical capabilities. Because they cost money, Tsouli turned to the Internet to raise money. With a partner, he purchased stolen credit card numbers on various online forums and used them to charge more than $3.5 million. He also laundered money through several online gambling sites by

Errors Put National Security at Risk

Sometimes human error rather than a malicious hacker can put national security at risk. When governments store sensitive information online or in electronic databases, they are vulnerable to data breaches that release that information to unintended parties. Sensitive information can fall into the wrong hands because of lost laptops, software that has not been updated for security fixes, or employee mistakes in online security procedures.

In 2009 a Transportation Security Administration (TSA) employee accidentally posted a manual for airport screening procedures on a public website. The manual included details on how TSA agents screen passengers; check for explosive devices; and handle CIA agents, diplomats, and law enforcement officials, as well as the technical settings for the metal and explosive detectors used at airports across the United States.

Also in 2009 an external hard drive that contained one terabyte of data from the Clinton administration went missing from NARA. In addition to more than 100,000 Social Security numbers and home addresses for people who visited or worked at the White House, the drive contained details on the security procedures used by the Secret Service at the White House.

using the stolen credit cards to gamble and then transferred any winnings to bank accounts he set up.

Online charities are another avenue terrorist organizations use to raise money. Some are existing organizations that terrorists have penetrated, diverting money away from legitimate causes. Others disguise their intent behind vague mission statements such as saying their fundraising is for humanitarian purposes. In one example, the Foundation for Human Rights and Freedoms and Humanitarian Relief claims to be an entirely peaceful organization. Yet the Intelligence and Terrorism Information Center, an Israel-based organization, says that while this organization does have philanthropic activities, it is also a supporter of the terrorist group Hamas. General Richard Myers, former chair of the US Joint Chiefs of Staff, says that donors need to be cautious about the charitable organizations they support. "A lot of wealthy benefactors providing donations for humanitarian relief don't know what they're funding. They think they're doing something for welfare and educa-tion,"[54] he says. In reality, some of the do-nations may be used to support extremist or terrorist groups.

The anonymity of the Internet makes it difficult for law enforcement officials to ef-fectively monitor and track terrorist fund-raising. Cybercriminals such as Tsouli can hide their identity by using stolen credit cards and identities, never using their real identity. With a little technical knowledge, cyberterrorists can hide their computer's IP addresses by using certain software and proxy servers. In addition, as governments shut down charities or websites linked to terrorist fund-raising, terrorist organizations can easily open a new site the next day in a different name.

> "There's a whole new wave of cyber attacks being launched right now at the U.S. government and businesses from very sophisticated threat sources."[58]
>
> — Ronald Ross, a government computer scientist.

Fighting Cyberterrorism

With thousands of daily attacks on government, military, and corpo-rate computer systems, governments are taking the threat of cyberter-rorism seriously. In May 2009 President Obama announced a govern-ment strategy for cyberattacks. He created a new White House office to be led by a cybersecurity coordinator. The office will coordinate all cybersecurity policies and coordinate a response in the event of a cyber-attack. According to Obama:

> From now on, our digital infrastructure—the networks and com-puters we depend on every day—will be treated as they should be: as a strategic national asset. Protecting this infrastructure will be a national security priority. We will ensure that these networks are secure, trustworthy, and resilient. We will deter, prevent, de-tect, and defend against attacks and recover quickly from any disruptions or damage.[55]

In addition, Secretary of Defense Robert Gates announced the creation of the US Cyber Command in 2009. He appointed US Army general Keith B. Alexander in 2010 as the Cyber Command's first leader. The Cyber Command's mission is to organize and train for digital war and to oversee offensive and defensive operations. "Given our increasing dependency on cyberspace, this new command will bring together the resources of the department to address vulnerabilities and meet the ever-growing array of cyber threats to our military systems,"[56] says Gates.

Deputy Defense Secretary William J. Lynn III noted the critical importance of cybersecurity to national defense in a 2009 speech to the Center for Strategic & International Studies:

> Just like our national dependence, there is simply no exaggerating our military dependence on our information networks: the command and control of our forces, the intelligence and logistics on which they depend, the weapons technologies we develop and field—they all depend on our computer systems and networks. Indeed, our 21st century military simply cannot function without them.[57]

Defense Contractors Bid on Cybersecurity

According to Alexander, head of Cyber Command, Pentagon systems are attacked 250,000 times an hour or 6 million times per day. The attacks come from a variety of sources, including foreign intelligence agents, criminal organizations, and individual hackers looking to make trouble. "It's an enormous problem that has been creeping up on us," said Ronald Ross, a government computer scientist who develops security guidelines for federal agencies and government contractors. "There's a whole new wave of cyber attacks being launched right now at the U.S. government and businesses from very sophisticated threat sources."[58]

With the volume of attacks escalating, the government has partnered with some traditional defense contractors to produce cyberwarfare tools and defenses. In one example, the Boeing Company is providing products to various government agencies for cyberdefense and cyberoffense. One Boeing product purchased by the US Department of Defense includes a system that monitors and alerts network administrators to potential intruders. "We expect to grow in this area with new facilities, new capabilities,"[59] said Jeff Trauberman, vice president of business development in Boeing's Network and Space Systems division. Cybersecurity is considered by analysts to be a growth industry, with estimates of $10 billion to $14 billion in available contracts. Confidential contract awards could double that amount.

The operational center of the US military, the Pentagon near Washington, DC, experiences 6 million attacks per day on its computer systems. The culprits in these attacks include foreign intelligence agents, criminal organizations, and individual hackers.

Early Warning Systems

In addition to efforts by defense contractors, developers in Washington State are working on an early warning system, the Public Regional Information Security Event Management (PRISEM) system. The system would alert local and state agencies if computers and networks are attacked in any way, from botnet attacks on desktop computers to full cyberattacks from terrorists. The city of Seattle already uses a security alert system that compiles security event information from its multiple network sources and provides a real-time analysis of the network threat.

Under the statewide PRISEM system, multiple communities and agencies would transmit data to central aggregation points. There it would be shared with participants across the state. The analysis data would also be shared with the federal government's Department of Homeland Security. Sharing information about security threats in one part of the state could help others. "Suppose I get an alert about suspected botnet infections on some desktops. We all need to know that,"[60] says Michael Hamilton, CISO of Seattle.

> "Over the next 20 to 30 years, cyber-attacks will increasingly become a component of war."[62]
>
> — William Crowell, a former deputy director of the National Security Agency.

If implemented, Washington's early warning system would be the first of its kind in the United States. If successful, it could become a model for other states and the federal government. Hamilton believes that once people see the success of the Washington system, it will inspire more cooperation between public and private entities to share information to combat cybersecurity threats. "It's a shared 'community watch' for cyber-threats,"[61] says Hamilton.

Cyberwar

Some people are concerned that the Internet and the digital world may soon be used by nations as a part of war. According to the McAfee *Virtual Criminology Report 2009*, politically motivated cyberattacks on governments and countries are increasing. When a cyberattack steals information or loads a virus onto a national computer system, it can threaten the national and economic security of many countries around the world. "Over the next 20 to 30 years, cyber-attacks will increasingly become a component of war," says William Crowell, a former deputy director of the National Security Agency. "What I can't foresee is whether networks will be so pervasive and unprotected that cyber war operations will stand alone."[62]

In addition to government and military targets, private businesses are vulnerable to nation-based cyberattacks. Public companies, financial markets, and electric power companies are some of the potential targets in a cyberwar. If they were to fall victim to a cyberattack or virus, entire systems crashing could create national disarray. Targeting these nonmilitary institutions challenges traditional rules of war but may become more common.

> **"The harsh reality is that (information technology) has become a tool for cybercrime and cyberterrorism. Cybersecurity must become a cornerstone of every aspect of keeping ourselves, our countries and our world safe."[65]**
>
> — Hamadoun Touré, secretary-general of the United Nations International Telecommunication Union.

Even though cyberattacks are occurring on a daily basis and have the potential to do serious damage, many countries are hesitant to admit or share information about the attacks. According to Scott Weber, former counsel to President George W. Bush's homeland security secretary Michael Chertoff, countries walk a fine line between sharing information about cyberterrorism and giving away too much national defense information and strategies for combating cyberterrorism.

International Cooperation

As cyberthreats increase, many believe that international cooperation is the only way to fight cyberterrorism effectively. Alexander Ntoko is a cybersecurity expert at the International Telecommunication Union, a United Nations agency for information and communications technology issues. He has been working on international cyberspace rules through the United Nations. "An international treaty is desirable and necessary," Ntoko told reporters. "However, its scope needs to take into account the broad nature of the threats, crimes, vulnerabilities, and attacks."[63]

Yet while participants agree that international cooperation is needed, it is difficult to achieve in practice. "There are certain innate limitations to the (international) discussions," says Weber. "The intelligence communities are using warfare . . . to hack into other countries' critical infrastructure. These are things that many countries are doing as part of their intelligence gathering and yet none of them will want to admit it in public."[64]

The Internet has transformed the way people live their lives, communicate, and do business. At the same time, the digital world has given rise to new threats to international peace and national security. In a speech to government authorities and technology experts from more than 30 nations, Hamadoun Touré, secretary-general of the International Telecommunication Union, urges members to cooperate to better fight cyberterrorism. "The harsh reality is that (information technology) has become a tool for cybercrime and cyberterrorism. Cybersecurity must become a cornerstone of every aspect of keeping ourselves, our countries and our world safe,"[65] says Touré.

Chapter Five

The Future of Online Security

Keeping up with rapid changes in digital technology and online security is no easy task. The Internet changes constantly, as do the ways in which people use it. Over time, new digital technologies will also require new forms of online security. Hackers, cyberterrorists, and other criminals are continually evolving methods to bypass the latest online security measures. All of these changes present new and varied opportunities for data breaches.

In addition, the nature of cyberthreats is shifting. Early computer viruses were usually launched by individual hackers who wanted to create chaos and gain fame. However, more recent cyberattacks have been growing more sophisticated and organized. Usually, they have been set into motion by criminals seeking information they can use for profit, such as credit card numbers, bank account access, and passwords.

The Smartphone Threat

Mobile technology is an emerging arena for online security threats. As global sales of smartphones and other mobile technologies skyrocket, more people will use mobile devices to access bank accounts, e-mail, and social networking sites. Business users will log on to corporate networks to access business data and services from mobile platforms.

As a result, experts are predicting that more malware and other security threats will spread through mobile devices. "So far, malware on mobile phones has not been a major issue," says Arun Chandrasekaran, a research manager at Frost & Sullivan, a global business consulting company in Sydney, Australia. "But mobile security has the potential to be exploited quite easily by hackers, and it's only a matter of time before it starts happening."[66] In one example, a virus infected more than 1 million mobile phones in China in 2010. Masked as an antivirus application, the malware allowed hackers to access the phones' SIM cards and send spam text messages to people on the phones' contact lists.

According to the *Cisco 2010 Annual Security Report*, hackers have already begun shifting their focus from Windows-based PCs to smart-phones, tablet computers, and mobile platforms in general. "If the bad guys can get a link to arrive on your phone, disguised as if it's coming from Facebook, and get you to click on it, they've got you. It's just as

Experts say that hackers have begun to shift their focus from personal computers to the proliferation of smartphones, tablet computers, and other mobile technologies. Mobile apps are one area that security experts will be watching in the future.

trivial to install a banking Trojan on your smartphone, including iPhones and Droids, as it is on a PC,"[67] says Fred Touchette, a researcher for App-River, an Internet security company.

Risky Mobile Apps

In particular the mobile apps store is a new way for hackers to reach millions of users quickly. In 2010 millions of users discovered that free wallpaper apps downloaded from the Android market were collecting information such as mobile phone numbers and subscriber identification codes. This personal information was then being forwarded to an unknown recipient in China. "Third-party mobile apps are emerging as a serious threat vector," says Horacio Zambrano, product line manager for Cisco. "No one is looking at these apps and determining what is a 'good app' or a 'bad app.'"[68]

In addition to suspicious apps, apps from legitimate companies may also be an online security risk. "A lot of the new applications coming into the market are developed by small firms, and they are not looking into the security implications of some of their applications,"[69] says Chandrasekaran. Andrew Hoog, chief investigative officer for viaForensics, a Chicago company that specializes in securing mobile applications, agrees that many popular mobile apps have security vulnerabilities. His company tested several mobile apps to see whether they securely stored user names, passwords, and other sensitive data. "We've tested about 50 popular mobile apps . . . and I believe only two or three passed the initial audit," says Hoog. "While I see some risk in rogue apps, the larger concern is perfectly legitimate apps that put consumers' sensitive data at risk through poor development, testing and security practices."[70]

Wi-Fi Insecurity

Computing on the run through Wi-Fi spots at the local coffee shop, bookstore, or other public place may also lead to more online security risks and data breaches. Until recently, only determined and talented hackers could spy on users while they used laptops or smartphones at Wi-Fi hot spots. But a free software program called Firesheep, released in October 2010, has made it simple for millions to spy on users of unsecured Wi-Fi networks. When a user enters a password on a website like Facebook or eBay, it is usually encrypted. However, the web browser's cookie, which is a piece of code that identifies a computer, site settings, or other personal information, is usually not encrypted. Firesheep takes that cookie and allows hackers to pretend to be the user on the website. "I released Firesheep to show that a core and widespread issue in Web site security is being ignored," says Eric Butler, a freelance software developer in Seattle who created the program. "It points out the lack of end-to-end encryption."[71] In the three months since Firesheep's release, more than 1 million users have downloaded the spying software.

Firesheep's tactics do not work on sites that use end-to-end encryption, a type of secure coding, throughout a user's session. These sites usually have a web address that starts with "https" instead of "http." While some sites, including PayPal and many banks, use end-to-end encryption,

> **"Mobile security has the potential to be exploited quite easily by hackers, and it's only a matter of time before it starts happening."**[66]
>
> — Arun Chandrasekaran, a research manager at Frost & Sullivan, a global business consulting company in Sydney, Australia.

many others do not. "The usual reason Web sites give for not encrypting all communication is that it will slow down the site and would be a huge engineering expense," says Chris Palmer, technology director at the Electronic Frontier Foundation, an electronic rights advocacy group based in San Francisco. "Yes, there are operational hurdles, but they are solvable."[72]

According to some experts, the safest solution may simply be for users to limit the ways they use the Internet in public Wi-Fi hot spots. "I tell people that if you're doing things with sensitive data, don't do it at a Wi-Fi hot spot. Do it at home,"[73] says Bill Pennington, chief strategy officer with WhiteHat Security, a website risk management firm.

Cloud Computing

Another emerging technology trend is cloud computing. Before cloud computing, users stored files and programs on their local computer hard drive or network servers. With cloud computing, users store data and use applications hosted on a third party's servers. Users load a single

Investigating Wireless Hackers

When investigating online security breaches that result from hackers, investigators often hit a dead end when they trace a cybercriminal's digital footprint back to a wireless network. Many times, cybercriminals will log on to the poorly protected wireless networks of neighbors or businesses to operate. Investigators can trace their cyberattacks back to the wireless network, but not to the specific mobile device connected to that network. Without the ability to locate the device connected to the wireless network, investigations may stall.

A new tool from the cybersecurity company Digital Certainty attempts to solve this problem for investigators. Wi-Fi Investigator is a wireless device locator that allows police to find the physical location of active wireless devices. When a cyberthief logs onto a wireless network, Wi-Fi Investigator can conduct surveillance on his or her activity. It can also calculate GPS coordinates of the device's location, leading police right to the thief.

application onto their computer, usually something as simple as a web browser. Then they log on to a web-based service that hosts all the programs they need, such as e-mail, word processing, or complex data applications. Remote machines owned by the cloud computing company store data and run and maintain the applications.

One of the main benefits of cloud computing is that local users and computers do not have to spend thousands of dollars on the latest hardware and software. Instead they can log on to the cloud via the Internet, access up-to-date programs, and store their data with no space limitations. For companies, cloud computing allows computer systems to be upgraded easily and cost effectively as the business grows and changes. Many users are already using a form of cloud computing if they have a web-based e-mail service such as Hotmail, Yahoo!, or Google. They log in to their e-mail from any location. The software and storage is not on their local computer; instead it is in the cloud's network.

Although there are many benefits to using cloud computing, there are also several significant security risks. This centralized data repository for multiple companies or individuals becomes an inviting target for hackers. If they can breach the cloud, they have access to a large amount of data. Gary Loveland, a principal at PricewaterhouseCoopers and head of the firm's global security practice, says: "Cyber criminals choose to attack targets where their efforts can yield the highest benefit, and large cloud providers are big targets with potential treasure troves of data that can be sold on the black market. Further, cloud providers are often connected to many corporate networks and, if penetrated, provide a good launching point for distributed attacks."[74]

Cloud Security

While some of the larger cloud computing services employ many layers of security to protect user data from hackers, other providers are not as security conscious. A survey by Symantec and the Ponemon Institute in April 2010 found that most businesses lacked the procedures, policies, and tools to make sure the data they put into the cloud was secure. Only 27 percent of companies surveyed had a procedure to approve cloud applications that used confidential information. More than 50 percent simply took a cloud computing provider's word that it employed adequate security procedures. "Cloud computing holds a great deal of promise . . . but our study reveals a disturbing lack of concern for the security of sensitive corporate and personal information as companies rush to join in on the trend,"[75] says Larry Ponemon, chair and founder of the Ponemon Institute.

> "I tell people that if you're doing things with sensitive data, don't do it at a Wi-Fi hot spot. Do it at home."[73]
>
> — Bill Pennington, chief strategy officer with WhiteHat Security, a website risk management firm.

Storing data in a cloud means that users and companies are relying on the cloud provider's controls to ensure that data stays confidential. Online security experts recommend that users ask their cloud providers what is being done to ensure data privacy and segregation, where the data will be stored, and how it can be recovered in the event of a disaster.

In addition, cloud clients should ask their providers about the investigative support the provider will give in the event of hacking or other illegal activity. Gartner, a technology research and advisory company, warned in a June 2008 report on cloud computing:

> Cloud services are especially difficult to investigate, because logging and data for multiple customers may be co-located and may also be spread across an ever-changing set of hosts and data centers. If you cannot get a contractual commitment to support specific forms of investigation, along with evidence that the vendor has already successfully supported such activities, then your only safe assumption is that investigation and discovery requests will be impossible.[76]

Online security experts warn that one of the biggest mistakes that cloud users make is not asking about how the cloud provider screens its employees. Cloud employees have access to a company's sensitive data, but are outside the company's in-house control procedures. Chris Drake, CEO and founder of FireHost, a secure web hosting company, believes that it is critical for companies to understand how and if the cloud provider is screening its administrators. "At the end of the day, it comes down to the human factor," says Drake. "The human factor is still the biggest security threat."[77]

New Safeguards to Improve Online Security

To protect against more complex and powerful cyberthreats, individuals and organizations are looking to strengthen computer and Internet defenses. To slow down cyberrobberies, banks and other online financial institutions will use more knowledge-based authentication questions. These questions are an extra layer of security on top of traditional user

Wi-Fi service in coffee shops, bookstores, and other public places offers convenience as well as broadening Internet access. Experts say that Internet use at these spots also opens the door to identity theft.

names and passwords. The authentication questions may ask, "What is the name of your first pet?" or "What street did you grow up on?" The questions are designed to be so personal that it would be very difficult for a criminal impersonating a user to answer correctly. Doug Johnson, the American Bankers Association vice president of risk-management policy, says: "The questions are going to get more difficult over time. The threat is real, and (banks) are providing the tools to help customers protect themselves."[78]

Another potential new procedure is the use of a map to log on to secure sites. Because hackers and keystroke recording malware can easily steal traditional passwords, computer scientist Bill Cheswick designed a new type of password: clicking on a map. At the New York Institute of Technology Cyber Security Conference in 2010, Cheswick described how users would memorize a specific location on a satellite photo. The latitude and longitude coordinates of the location would be the user's access code. He says that drilling down through data on a digital map would create a nearly unbreakable password. Hackers and viruses can determine where the user's mouse clicks, but unless they also know what map the user is using and how far the user has zoomed in, the hackers cannot record the specific latitude and longitude that are the user's password. "The key idea is that you have a data set with very deep data, and you have to drill down," says Cheswick. "You could drill down on a map of anything. Probably better if it's a map of someplace you've never been, so you're not tempted to pick your childhood home. You could have a 10 digit latitude, and a 10-digit longitude, then you have a 20-digit password."[79]

> "Cyber criminals choose to attack targets where their efforts can yield the highest benefit, and large cloud providers are big targets with potential treasure troves of data that can be sold on the black market."[74]
>
> — Gary Loveland, a principal at PricewaterhouseCoopers and head of the firm's global security practice.

Some financial institutions are also considering implementing new technologies to make online transactions more secure. Handheld optical readers are one type of new technology that might better protect customers from cyberthieves. The size of a credit card, the optical reader fits into a wallet like a banking card. To use the card, the user presents the card in front of their computer screen. Optical sensors capture the card's data

Social Networks

Online social networking sites have opened new threats to online security. Malware attackers have starting to use social networking sites as launch pads, raising concerns that malicious code could spread quickly. The size of social networks and the trust a user places in messages from family and friends makes it an ideal place to spread malware. Experts estimate that Facebook and Twitter alone will have more than 700 million targets in 2011. If users clicks on tainted Facebook links, they might unknowingly download a program that infects their computers and installs malware.

According to Internet security experts, social network users can expect more threats to spread virally and infect everyone on a user's friend list. These viruses will most likely steal a user's personal information, which can then be used to obtain credit card and banking information. Alternately, stolen personal information could be sold on the black market to other cyberthieves.

to authorize banking transactions. No keypad strokes are needed. Using this type of verification device would help banks and users verify a secure transaction even if the customer's PC is infected with malware.

Training Cyberexperts

With online security growing in importance, computer experts are needed more than ever to protect cyberassets. According to the Bureau of Labor Statistics, more than 2 million new technology-related jobs are expected to be created by 2018. Some of the strong growth potential areas include computer network administration, data-loss prevention, online security, and risk management.

To prepare students for careers in cybersecurity, Randy Marchany, a Virginia Tech IT security officer and cybersecurity specialist, has designed specialized camps for teens and young adults with strong computer skills. His US Cyber Challenge camps are part of an effort by the Defense Department to attract talented teens into cybersecurity careers. According to the camp's website, "The mission of the U.S. Cyber Challenge (USCC) is to significantly reduce the shortage in the cyber workforce by serving as the premier program to identify, recruit and place the next generation of cyber security professionals."[80]

The camps are held in several locations across the country. At Delaware's 2010 weeklong camp, 20 students participated in an intensive schedule of daily learning sessions, met with cyberexperts, and toured the Delaware State Police High Tech Crimes Lab. Topics covered included hacking, computer crime investigation techniques, and how to respond to cyberattacks. Organizers and participants believe the camp will help prepare talented young people for careers in cybersecurity. "We are a society that is increasingly dependent on computers and computer networks to do everything from shopping online and sending text messages to investing for retirement and emergency response," said Mark Pellegrini, a camp participant who is pursuing a PhD in computer engineering at the University of Delaware. "If we are going to be so dependent on computers for our daily needs, it is critical that we take steps to guarantee that they are reliable and secure."[81]

Federal Legislation

Amid growing concern over the United States' online vulnerability, lawmakers have proposed several bills in Congress regarding cybersecurity. One bill, proposed by Connecticut senator Joe Lieberman, is a wide-ranging piece of legislation improving the security of the nation's critical infrastructure, both in government and the private sector. It calls for automated continuous monitoring of systems and improved accountability for cybersecurity. The proposed act also calls for mandatory security controls for agency IT systems.

In addition, President Barack Obama released a cybersecurity plan in May 2011. The plan's recommendations include establishing a system of national data breach reporting, clarifying and standardizing penalties for computer criminals, and additional cybersecurity legislation. "The cyber security vulnerabilities in our government and critical infrastructure are a risk to national security, public safety and economic prosperity," said a White House statement. "The administration has responded to Congress' call for input on the cybersecurity legislation that our nation needs, and we look forward to engaging with Congress as they move forward on this issue."[82]

Cooperation Across Borders

The Internet has broken down borders around the world, allowing people from different states and countries to interact, do business, and communicate more easily than ever. At the same time, threats to online security can strike from anywhere, anytime. Gangs of cyberthieves do not need to be physically located together; instead they can operate from countries around the world. Law enforcement experts say that the key to fighting cybercrime is international cooperation.

In 2010 the FBI and law enforcement authorities from several countries worked together to disrupt an international cybertheft ring. The criminals infected computers with malware that captured passwords, account numbers, and other data used for online banking. With the stolen information, they attempted to steal $220 million. To stop the cybercrooks, the FBI worked closely with international agencies to identify and arrest suspects involved in the operation. Special Agent Weysan Dun, who worked on the case, said that despite the differences in time zones, geography, culture, and cyberlaws, the different countries were able to work together, which led to the successful bust.

While timely cooperation is important, Christopher Painter, deputy assistant director of the FBI's Cyber Division, says that laws against cybercrimes need to be consistent from state to state and country to country. If not, criminals will simply learn to base their operations in jurisdictions where penalties are the least severe. "The bottom line is to make sure there are consequences for criminal cyber actions and similar consequences everywhere. The bad guys need to know there is no free ride,"[83] says Painter.

> "If we are going to be so dependent on computers for our daily needs, it is critical that we take steps to guarantee that they are reliable and secure."[81]
>
> — Mark Pellegrini, a US Cyber Challenge camp participant who is pursuing a PhD in computer engineering at the University of Delaware.

International Treaty

In a step toward international cooperation, the Council of Europe introduced a treaty called the Convention on Cybercrime in 2001. A decade later, countries still use the treaty as the primary guidance for international cooperation on cybercrime. The treaty establishes guidelines for sharing data between governments in cases of bank fraud, identity theft, child pornography, phishing, and other cases of online organized crime. Forty-six countries, including the United States, have signed the treaty.

Some countries, like Russia, are reluctant to sign the international treaty. Russia, considered a major source of cybercrime, says it does not want to give foreign law-enforcement agents unlimited access to its web data, which the treaty requires. Alternately, Russia has proposed an arms-control treaty where all nations would agree not to use cyberweapons. Yet critics point out that it would be nearly impossible to define cyberweapons and determine whether a government or an individual hacker was responsible for a cyberattack.

> "If we're going to protect our networks, our infrastructure, our economy and our families, we have to go after cyber criminals wherever they may be—and it must be an international effort."[84]
>
> — Senator Kirsten Gillibrand of New York.

To ensure that all countries are taking cybercrime seriously, US lawmakers introduced the International Cybercrime Reporting and Cooperation Act in 2010. If passed, the act would require the president to report annually to Congress on cybercrime emanating from each country and the effectiveness of that country's legal and law enforcement systems. It would also identify countries of cyberconcern, where there is significant, credible evidence that a pattern of cybercrime against the United States exists. If the country did not actively address its cybercrime, the United States could impose a variety of economic sanctions. "If we're going to protect our networks, our infrastructure, our economy and our families, we have to go after cyber criminals wherever they may be—and it must be an international effort," says Senator Kirsten Gillibrand of New York, one of the bill's cosponsors. "Our legislation will make America safer by getting tough on cybercrime globally, and coordinating with our partners in the international community."[84]

A Digital Age

All over the world, people are logging onto computers and the Internet. Access to information and communication is easier than ever. Surfing the Internet on laptops, computers, and mobile devices, people can read the latest news and research almost any topic in minutes. With e-mail, instant messaging, and social networking, people thousands of miles apart can communicate, share ideas, and learn about different cultures.

At the same time, the Internet and the digital age have opened the door to new vulnerabilities and problems with online security. Valuable information can be lost, stolen, and changed. Cybercriminals hack into corporate computer systems, stealing databases of customers' personal information or corporate secrets. Cyberspies can use the Internet and digital technology to disrupt the operation of websites, companies, and governments.

To minimize these risks, governments, law enforcement agencies, and communities around the world are working to educate users and design new procedures and technologies that better ensure online security. Says President Obama:

> The Internet has transformed how we communicate and do business, opening up markets, and connecting our society as never before. But it has also led to new challenges, like online fraud and identity theft, that harm consumers and cost billions of dollars each year. By making online transactions more trustworthy and better protecting privacy, we will prevent costly crime, we will give businesses and consumers new confidence, and we will foster growth and untold innovation.[85]

Source Notes

Introduction: Data Breach

1. Quoted in Janet Lavelle, "Insurer Health Net Says It Had Huge Data Breach," *San Diego Union Tribune*, March 14, 2011. www.signonsandiego.com.
2. Quoted in Lavelle, "Insurer Health Net Says It Had Huge Data Breach."
3. Quoted in Margaret Collins, "Medical Identity Theft Growing, and at No Small Price," *Austin (TX) Statesman*, March 27, 2010. www.statesman.com.
4. Quoted in Matt Kettmann, "Just the Hackers You Need," *Santa Barbara Independent*, December 16, 2010. www.independent.com.
5. Quoted in Kettmann, "Just the Hackers You Need."

Chapter One: Going Online: A Growing Risk

6. Quoted in Ryan Singel, "Probe Targets Archives' Handling of Data on 70 Million Vets," *Wired*, October 1, 2009. www.wired.com.
7. Quoted in Carolyn Salazar, "How Dangerous Is Online Banking?," MSN Money, January 28, 2009. http://articles.moneycentral.msn.com.
8. Quoted in comScore, "Global Internet Audience Surpasses 1 Billion Visitors," press release, January 23, 2009. www.comscore.com.
9. Quoted in Marketing Charts, "Online Security a Growing Concern for Americans," July 28, 2008. www.marketingcharts.com.
10. Quoted in Trend Micro, "Employees Put Personal Online Security and Interests Above Their Company's," press release, May 10, 2010. http://trendmicro.mediaroom.com.
11. Quoted in Rebecca Neal, "Cybersecurity Concerns Grow for Federal CIOs," *Federal Times*, March 23, 2010. www.federaltimes.com.
12. Quoted in Bill Turque, "Data About Students Dispersed in Breach," *Washington Post*, May 12, 2009. www.washingtonpost.com.
13. Quoted in Cliff Edwards and Michael Riley, "Sony Breach Exposes Users to Identity Theft as Credit-Card Threat Recedes," Bloomberg, May 3, 2011. www.bloomberg.com.

14. Robert Knake, "Cyberterrorism Hype v. Fact," Council on Foreign Relations, February 16, 2010. www.cfr.org.
15. Quoted in Katherine Walsh, "The ERP Security Challenge: Q&A," *CSO Online*, January 8, 2008. www.csoonline.com.

Chapter Two: Identity Theft

16. Quoted in Jennifer Waters, "Identity Fraud Nightmare: One Man's Story," MarketWatch, February 10, 2010. www.marketwatch.com.
17. Quoted in Waters, "Identity Fraud Nightmare."
18. Quoted in Andrea Neal, "Guarding Against Identity Theft," *Saturday Evening Post*, May 2007, p. 48.
19. Quoted in Waters, "Identity Fraud Nightmare."
20. Quoted in Neal, "Guarding Against Identity Theft," p. 48.
21. Quoted in John Blake, "The Hidden Cost of Identity Theft," CNN.com, December 7, 2009. http://articles.cnn.com.
22. Quoted in WKYC.com, "Posting Pictures Online Raises Risk of Child Identity Theft," April 14, 2011. www.wkyc.com.
23. Quoted in WKYC.com, "Posting Pictures Online Raises Risk of Child Identity Theft."
24. Quoted in Walecia Konrad, "Medical Problems Could Include Identity Theft," *New York Times*, June 12, 2009. www.nytimes.com.
25. Quoted in Collins, "Medical Identity Theft Growing, and at No Small Price."
26. Quoted in René Millman, "New York Enacts Data Break Law," *SC Magazine*, August 15, 2005. www.scmagazineus.com.
27. Quoted in David McGuire, "Bush Signs Identity Theft Bill," *Washington Post*, July 15, 2004. www.washingtonpost.com.
28. Quoted in Federal Trade Commission, "The President's Identity Theft Task Force Releases Comprehensive Strategic Plan to Combat Identity Theft," press release, April 23, 2007. www.ftc.gov.
29. Quoted in Jeff Gelles, "Guarding Against Identity Theft Requires Much Vigilance," *Philadelphia Inquirer*, May 5, 2011. www.philly.com.

Chapter Three: Securing Company Networks

30. Quoted in Kim Zetter, "Google Hack Attack Was Ultra Sophisticated, New Details Show," *Wired*, January 14, 2010. www.wired.com.

31. Quoted in John Markoff, "Cyberattack on Google Said to Hit Password System," *New York Times*, April 19, 2010. www.nytimes.com.
32. Quoted in Fahmida Y. Rashid, "Average Data Breach Cost Rises to $7.2 Million per Incident: Survey," eWeek.com, March 8, 2011. www.eweek.com.
33. Quoted in Liana B. Baker and Jim Finkle, "Sony PlayStation Suffers Massive Data Breach," Reuters, April 26, 2011. www.reuters.com.
34. Quoted in Edwards and Riley, "Sony Breach Exposes Users to Identity Theft as Credit-Card Threat Recedes."
35. Quoted in Michael Riley and Sara Forden, "China-Based Hacking of DuPont Was One of Undisclosed Google-Type Attacks," Bloomberg, March 8, 2011. www.bloomberg.com.
36. Quoted in Riley and Forden, "China-Based Hacking of DuPont Was One of Undisclosed Google-Type Attacks."
37. Quoted in Rashid, "Average Data Breach Cost Rises to $7.2 Million per Incident."
38. Quoted in Starr Keshet, "Cyber Crime Costs Corporate America Billions," TG Daily, July 26, 2010. www.tgdaily.com.
39. Quoted in Larry Greenemeier, "FTC Issues Warning to Plug P2P Security Holes," *Scientific American*, February 23, 2010. www.scientificamerican.com.
40. Quoted in Federal Trade Commission, "Widespread Data Breaches Uncovered by FTC Probe," press release, February 22, 2010. www.ftc.gov.
41. J. Robert Beyster, "The Cybersecurity Challenge: Corporate Cybercrime and Government Cybercrime," Foundation for Enterprise Development, July 28, 2009. www.beyster.com.
42. Quoted in Antony Savvas, "Merck Moves to Improve System Security and Compliance," *CSO Online*, January 29, 2011. www.csoonline.com.
43. Quoted in Mark Cox, "Educating Employees Key in Web 2.0 Security Strategy," eChannelLine.com, August 2, 2010. www.echannelline.com.
44. Michael Farnum, "Security Awareness Training Does Not Have to Be Hard," *Computerworld*, December 14, 2006. http://blogs.computerworld.com.
45. Quoted in Kenneth Corbin, "Senate Dems Push Data Breach Bill," eSecurity Planet.com, August 9, 2010. www.esecurityplanet.com.

46. Quoted in George Hulme, "Data Breach Fines Can Risk More Harm than Good, Experts Say," *CSO Online*, April 21, 2011. www.csoonline.com.

47. Quoted in Gautham Nagesh, "Industry Opposes Federal Role in Private Cybersecurity," Hill, March 8, 2011. http://thehill.com.

48. Quoted in Dana Gardner, "Expert Panel: As Cyber Security Risks Grow, Architected Protection and Best Practices Must Keep Pace," hp.com, February 28, 2011. http://h30501.www3.hp.com.

Chapter Four: National Security and Cyberterrorism

49. Quoted in Jason Fisher, "Cyberwar Enters a New Phase: Stuxnet and Iran," *Foreign Policy Digest*, February 1, 2011. www.foreignpolicydigest.org.

50. Quoted in William J. Broad, John Markoff, and David E. Sanger, "Israeli Test on Worm Called Crucial in Iran Nuclear Delay," *New York Times*, January 15, 2011. www.nytimes.com.

51. Quoted in Ellen Nakashima, "FBI Director Warns of 'Rapidly Expanding' Cyberterrorism Threat," *Washington Post*, March 4, 2010. www.washingtonpost.com.

52. Cyberterrorism Defense Initiative, "Cyberterrorism Defense Analysis Center." www.cyberterrorismcenter.org.

53. Quoted in J. Nicholas Hoover, "NASA Servers at High Risk of Cyber Attack," *InformationWeek*, March 30, 2011. www.informationweek.com.

54. Quoted in Alexander Christie-Miller and James Hider, "Turkish Charity That Sent Aid Convoy to Gaza 'Has Links to Terrorism,'" *Times Online*, June 3, 2010. www.timesonline.co.uk.

55. President Barack Obama, "Obama's Remarks on CyberSecurity," *New York Times*, May 29, 2010. www.nytimes.com.

56. Quoted in US Department of Defense, "DOD Announces First U.S. Cyber Command and First U.S. CYBERCOM Commander," news release, May 21, 2010. www.defense.gov.

57. Quoted in Donna Miles, "Gates Establishes New Cyber Subcommand," US Department of Defense, June 24, 2009. www.defense.gov.

58. Quoted in Bill Lambrecht, "Boeing Among Defense Contractors Fighting Cyberterrorism," *Chicago Tribune*, June 28, 2010. http://articles.chicagotribune.com.

59. Quoted in Lambrecht, "Boeing Among Defense Contractors Fighting Cyberterrorism."
60. Quoted in Ellen Messmer, "Cyberattack-Alert System Could Be Model for U.S.," *Network World*, March 8, 2011. www.network world.com.
61. Quoted in Messmer, "Cyberattack-Alert System Could Be Model for U.S."
62. Quoted in Xinhua, "Are Cyber Security and International Cooperation at Odds?," China.org, December 19, 2009. www.china.org.cn.
63. Quoted in Xinhua, "Are Cyber Security and International Cooperation at Odds?"
64. Quoted in Xinhua, "Are Cyber Security and International Cooperation at Odds?"
65. Quoted in Julia Zappei, "Experts Warn of Cyberterrorism Threat," *USA Today*, May 21, 2008. www.usatoday.com.

Chapter Five: The Future of Online Security

66. Quoted in Sonia Kolesnikov-Jessop, "Hackers Go After the Smartphone," *New York Times*, February 13, 2011. www.nytimes.com.
67. Quoted in Byron Acohido, "Zeus Banking Trojan Attacks Spread to Social Networks, Smartphones," *USA Today*, October 8, 2010. http://content.usatoday.com.
68. Quoted in Cisco, *"Cisco 2010 Annual Security Report."* www.cisco.com.
69. Quoted in Kolesnikov-Jessop, "Hackers Go After the Smartphone."
70. Quoted in Kolesnikov-Jessop, "Hackers Go After the Smartphone."
71. Quoted in Kate Murphy, "New Hacking Tools Pose Bigger Threats to Wi-Fi Users," *New York Times*, February 16, 2011. www.nytimes.com.
72. Quoted in Murphy, "New Hacking Tools Pose Bigger Threats to Wi-Fi Users."
73. Quoted in Murphy, "New Hacking Tools Pose Bigger Threats to Wi-Fi Users."
74. Quoted in Bob Violino, "PwC Interview: Security Lessons in the Cloud," *CSO Online*, February 1, 2011. www.csoonline.com.
75. Quoted in Symantec, "Fewer than One in Ten Companies Evaluate Vendors or Train Employees on Cloud Security," press release, April 5, 2010. www.symantec.com.

76. Quoted in Jon Brodkin, "Gartner: Seven Cloud-Computing Security Risks," InfoWorld, July 2, 2008. www.infoworld.com.

77. Quoted in Chris Morris, "New Security Concerns Floating Around in Cloud Computing," Switched, April 29, 2010. www.switched.com.

78. Quoted in Byron Acohido, "Banks Seek Customers' Help to Stop Online Thieves," *USA Today*, July 30, 2010. www.usatoday.com.

79. Quoted in Stuart Fox, "Future Online Password Could Be a Map," MSNBC.com, September 20, 2010. www.msnbc.msn.com.

80. US Cyber Challenge. www.uscyberchallenge.org.

81. Quoted in State of Delaware, "First Class Graduates from US Cyber Challenge Delaware Camp," August 13, 2010. http://governor.delaware.gov.

82. Quoted in David Jackson, "Obama Team Unveils Cybersecurity Plan," *USA Today*, May 12, 2011. http://content.usatoday.com.

83. Quoted in *North Country Gazette* (New York), "International Cooperation Needed to Fight Cyber Crime," January 14, 2009. www.northcountrygazette.org.

84. Quoted in Senator Kirsten Gillibrand, "Cybercrime Costs NY Businesses Approximately $4.6 Billion Each Year—Gillibrand, Hatch Introduce First of Its Kind Measure to Bolster Cybersecurity in America," press release, March 23, 2010. http://gillibrand.senate.gov.

85. Quoted in White House, "Administration Releases Strategy to Protect Online Consumers and Support Innovation and Fact Sheet on National Strategy for Trusted Identities in Cyberspace," press release, April 15, 2011. www.whitehouse.gov.

Facts About Online Security

- According to the Ponemon Institute's 2010 annual study of the costs of data loss, malicious attacks are some of the most expensive to remedy, costing companies an average of $318 per data record breached.

- Over 150 million US citizens are connected to the Internet, says the GAO.

- According to a 2010 report from *Consumer Reports*, over a 6-month period, 8 million US households had serious problems with spyware, causing $1.2 billion in damage.

- Nearly three-quarters (71 percent) of adults report managing at least one financial services account online, according to Mintel. The average American manages three financial services accounts via e-mail and the web.

- A June 2010 survey by Symantec of 2,152 global small to medium-sized businesses found that 73 percent reported they were the victims of cyberattacks in the past year and 42 percent said they had lost confidential or proprietary information.

- A TechAmerica survey released in 2010 of 45 federal CIOs and information resources managers found that 54 percent said their agencies are actively adopting cloud computing.

- A Trend Micro 2010 survey found that 36 percent of US end-users said loss of personal information was their top concern about viruses; yet only 29 percent expressed concern over the loss of corporate data due to viruses.

- Approximately 1 out of 10 users in a Trend Micro 2010 survey admitted to overriding their corporate security in order to access restricted websites.

- Across all countries, 60 percent of mobile workers versus 44 percent of stationary workers admitted to having sent out company confidential information via instant messaging, web mail, or social media applications, according to a Trend Micro 2010 survey.

- According to the Ponemon Institute, the cost of a data breach was $7.2 million in 2010, up from $6.8 million in 2009, with the average cost per compromised record in 2010 reaching $214, up 5 percent from 2009.

- A 2010 Ponemon Institute study found that quicker notification of data breaches cost companies more money. Companies that notified victims within 1 month of discovering the data breach paid $268 per record, while companies that took longer paid $174 per record.

- According to a Symantec 2010 survey, only 30 percent of respondents evaluated cloud computing vendors prior to employing their products.

- A Symantec 2010 survey found that only 19 percent of the respondents indicated that their company provides general data security training that discusses cloud applications.

- Research conducted by analysts at the Avast! Virus Lab has found that 1 out of every 8 attacks on computers now enters via a USB device.

- A 2011 study by CA Technologies and the Ponemon Institute found that less than 30 percent of cloud providers across the United States and Europe consider security as an important responsibility.

- There were more than 41,000 cyberattacks on government systems in 2010, a 39 percent increase over 2009, according to the Department of Homeland Security.

- In 2010, identity theft was the top consumer complaint received by the FTC.

- The Anti-Phishing Working Group says that more than 53 percent of desktop computers are infected with some type of malware.

- According to a 2009 Gallup crime survey, identity theft is Americans' top crime worry, with 66 percent of adults reporting that they worry frequently or occasionally about being a victim of identity theft.

Related Organizations

Anti-Phishing Working Group (APWG)
website: www.antiphishing.org

The APWG is an industry association focused on eliminating the identity theft and fraud that result from the growing problem of phishing and e-mail spoofing.

Bureau of Consumer Protection
600 Pennsylvania Ave. NW
Washington, DC 20580
phone: (202) 326-222
website: www.ftc.gov/bcp

A division of the Federal Trade Commission, the Bureau of Consumer Protection collects complaints about consumer fraud and identity theft and makes them available to law enforcement agencies across the country. Under the consumer information tab, the website has many publications regarding online security topics.

Federal Bureau of Investigation (FBI)— Cyber Crime Division
935 Pennsylvania Ave. NW
Washington, DC 20535-0001
phone: (202) 324-3000
website: www.fbi.gov/about-us/investigate/cyber/cyber

The FBI's Cyber Crime Division investigates high-tech crimes, including cyber-based terrorism, computer intrusions, and major cyberfrauds. Agents gather and share information and intelligence with public and private sector partners worldwide.

Identity Theft Resource Center (ITRC)
phone: (858) 693-7935
e-mail: itrc@idtheftcenter.org
website: www.idtheftcenter.org

The ITRC is a nonprofit organization dedicated to the understanding and prevention of identity theft. The center provides victim and consumer support and public education. The ITRC also advises governmental agencies, legislators, law enforcement, and businesses about the evolving and growing problem of identity theft.

Internet Crime Complaint Center (IC3)

website: www.ic3.org

IC3 is a partnership of the FBI, the National White Collar Crime Center, and the Bureau of Justice Assistance. IC3 receives complaints regarding cybercrime and coordinates investigatory efforts among law enforcement and regulatory agencies at the federal, state, local, and international level.

National Cyber-Forensics & Training Alliance (NCFTA)

2000 Technology Dr., Suite 450
Pittsburgh, PA 15219
phone: (412) 802-8000
fax: (412) 802-8510
e-mail: info@ncfta.net
website: www.ncfta.net

The NCFTA functions as a conduit between private industry and law enforcement to identify, mitigate, and neutralize cybercrime. NCFTA currently has formal partnerships/agreements with more than 40 US private-sector organizations and more than 15 US and international law enforcement or regulatory agencies.

National Cyber Security Division (NCSD)

Department of Homeland Security
Washington, DC 20528
phone: (202) 282-8000
website: www.dhs.gov/files/cybersecurity.shtm

A division of the Department of Homeland Security, the NCSD works collaboratively with public, private, and international entities to secure cyberspace and America's cyberassets.

Ponemon Institute

2308 US 31 North
Traverse City, MI 49686
phone: (231) 938-9900
fax: (231) 938-6215
e-mail: susan@ponemon.org
website: www.ponemon.org

The Ponemon Institute conducts independent research on privacy, data protection, and information security policy.

Privacy Rights Clearinghouse

3100 5th Ave., Suite B
San Diego, CA 92103
phone: (619) 298-3396
fax: (619) 298-5681
website: www.privacyrights.org

This organization is mainly concerned with the privacy rights of consumers. It offers information on issues such as identity theft, protecting the privacy of medical records, and ensuring that banks and other financial institutions do not divulge personal information to third parties without the consent of consumers.

The Public Voice

e-mail: coney@epic.org
website: http://thepublicvoice.org

An arm of the Electronic Privacy Information Center (EPIC), this organization focuses on the future of the Internet and the gathering of information worldwide. The website includes a number of articles and alerts about online privacy.

SANS Institute

phone: (301) 654-7267
e-mail: info@sans.org
website: www.sans.org

The SANS Institute is a nonprofit organization that offers computer security training, research, and resources. It develops, maintains, and makes available at no cost a large collection of research documents about various aspects of information security.

Symantec Corporation

World Headquarters
350 Ellis St.
Mountain View, CA 94043
phone: (650) 527-8000
website: www.symantec.com/security_response/index.jsp

Symantec is a provider of Internet security software. The Symantec Security Response website provides users with articles, tips, and information on the latest online security threats and issues.

US Postal Inspection Service (USPIS)

Criminal Investigations Service Center
Attn: Mail Fraud
222 S. Riverside Plaza, Suite 1250
Chicago, IL 60606-6100
phone: (877) 876-2455
website: https://postalinspectors.uspis.gov
The USPIS is the law enforcement arm of the US Postal Service. Many fraud schemes that originate over the Internet, such as auction fraud, involve payment or delivery via the US mail and are under the jurisdiction of the USPIS.

For Further Research

Books

Martin T. Biegelman, *Identity Theft Handbook: Detection, Prevention, and Security*. Hoboken, NJ: Wiley, 2009.

Bruce C. Brown, *How to Stop E-mail Spam, Spyware, Malware, Computer Viruses, and Hackers from Ruining Your Computer or Network: The Complete Guide for Your Home and Work*. Ocala, FL: Atlantic, 2009.

Johnny Cache, Joshua Wright, and Vincent Liu, *Hacking Exposed Wireless*. New York: McGraw-Hill, 2010.

Richard A. Clarke and Robert Knake, *Cyber War: The Next Threat to National Security and What to Do About It*. New York: Ecco, 2010.

Michael Davis, Sean Bodmer, and Aaron LeMasters, *Hacking Exposed: Malware & Rootkids Secrets & Solutions*. New York: McGraw-Hill, 2009.

Internet Sources

Bureau of Consumer Protection, "Medical Identity Theft," January 2010. www.ftc.gov/bcp/edu/pubs/consumer/idtheft/idt10.shtm.

———, "Minimizing the Effects of Malware on Your Computer," January 2008. www.ftc.gov/bcp/edu/pubs/consumer/tech/tec16.shtm.

Internet Crime Complaint Center, "2010 Internet Crime Report," 2011. www.ic3.gov/media/annualreport/2010_IC3Report.pdf.

Kathryn Zickuhr, "Generations and Their Gadgets," Pew Internet & American Life Project, February 3, 2011. www.pewinternet.org/Reports/2011/Generations-and-gadgets.aspx.

Websites

AnnualCreditReport.com (www.annualcreditreport.com/cra/index. jsp). Users who suspect they may be victims of identity theft may order a free annual credit report at this website.

Deter, Detect, Defend, Avoid ID Theft (www.ftc.gov/bcp/edu/micro sites/idtheft). The Federal Trade Commission's micro site is a resource to learn about the crime of identity theft. It provides detailed information to help users prevent and defend against identity theft.

Get Net Wise (www.getnetwise.org). Information and tutorials about the latest issues and concerns facing Internet users, including safety, wireless security, and spyware.

On Guard Online (www.onguardonline.gov). Provides practical tips from the federal government and technology industry to help users be on guard against Internet fraud, secure their computers, and protect their personal information.

Pew Internet & American Life Project (www.pewinternet.org). The Pew Internet & American Life Project is one of seven projects that make up the Pew Research Center. The project studies the Internet and digital technologies shaping the world today.

Stay Safe Online (www.staysafeonline.org). From the National Cyber Security Alliance, this site offers information and tools to help people use the Internet safely and securely at home, work, and school.

Index

Note: Boldface page numbers indicate illustrations.

Picture Credits

Cover: Thinkstock/Photodisc
Maury Aaseng: 6
AP Images: 11, 20, 24, 27, 33, 37, 47, 50, 61, 67
© David Brabyn/Corbis: 16
Thinkstock/Photodisc: 56

About the Author

Carla Mooney is the author of many books for young adults and children. She lives in Pittsburgh, Pennsylvania, with her husband and three children.